# Baseball For Boys

## By John M. Rosenburg

SUNVILLAGE
publications

www.sunvillagepublications.com

Baseball For Boys
By John M. Rosenburg

Copyright © 2010

No part of this publication may be reproduced, stored in a retrieval system or
transmitted in any form or by any means, electronic, mechanical, photocopying,
recording or otherwise, without prior written permission from the publisher.

www.sunvillagepublications.com

Cover design by www.WebCopyAlchemy.com

# ACKNOWLEDGEMENTS

Each year for more than 100 years, reams of copy have been written and published about the doings of baseball teams. The shelves of libraries and the archives of newspaper offices bulge with volumes of baseball statistics-batting averages, won-lost records, World Series results, etc.

Comparatively little information, however, has been committed to paper concerning the "how to play" aspect of the game. For the most part, the professional and amateur player has been taught the rudiments by word-of-mouth.

Being no exception, I wish to express my heartfelt gratitude to the scores of individuals who have passed their knowledge on to me and indirectly (and probably unknowingly) contributed to the ideas expressed in this work.

In particular, I want to identify my former coach at Hampton Bays High School (N. Y.), Samuel "Red" Manarel, and the talented men who coached me at Ithaca College— Ben Light, James A. "Bucky" Freeman and Major League manager Eddie Sawyer. A vote of thanks, too, goes to George Miner, with whom I worked at Johnson City High School (N. Y.).

I am also deeply indebted to three of my former college classmates and two latter-day colleagues who gave me considerable help and encouragement as I went through the pangs of developing the manuscript. This quintet includes Joseph Seavey, Richard B. Jesmajian, Charles "Tommy" Fitzgerald, Hugh A. Dever, Jr., and Richmond B. Williams.

Like all teachers, I have learned as much from my students as they have learned from me. This knowledge, for which I am most thankful, is threaded through the text. While I cannot recall all the names of the wonderful youngsters who played under me, rest assured that I can see their faces when I want to and remember the way this one could pound the curve to right, the way that one could drag a bunt and the way another could, with a graceful, feather-like touch, put the ball on a viciously sliding runner.

Some of the names, of course, still linger, as I hope they always will . . . Miller, Ramburg, Da Brescia, Heffren, Whittemore, York, O'Boyle, Whittaker, Possamato, Senia, Galatis, Surowka, Wyke, Caputo, Doyle, Collins, Biancardi, Di Orio, Horn, Dunphy, Silvanic, Rowan, Levane, Robinson, Laskoski, Johnston, Cappiello, Aimers . . . (as they say about charity drives, "committee still forming.")

I must further express my appreciation to Otto Echter, my illustrator, for his fine and original work and to my publisher for presenting the opportunity of getting this rather special material in print.

JMR

## DEDICATION

This book is dedicated to those individuals—whether they be sandlotters, fans or Major League owners—who have devoted time, money and energy to keeping baseball alive and growing and who, at the same time, have preserved the spirit and structure of the game, which we have known and revered in America for more than a century.

# TABLE OF CONTENTS

Chapter                                                                    Page

## Introduction

## PART I

### The Basic Skills

1.  Batting and Bunting...................................... 13
2.  Fielding and Throwing ..................................... 25
3.  Running the Bases and Sliding........................... 30

## PART II

### Individual Defense

4.   Pitching ................................................. 37
5.   Catching ................................................ 52
6.   First Base Play.......................................... 67
7.   Second Base Play ..................................... 72
8.   The Shortstop.......................... ................ 83
9.   Third Base Play ....................................... 88
10.  Outfield Play .........................................93

## PART HI

### Individual Offense

11.   Maneuvering on the Bases ...................................... 101

Chapter                                                   Page

12.  Leading Away and Stealing .................................. 107

13.  Reading the Signs ................................................111


## PART IV

### Team Defense

14.  The Bunt Defenses ................................................113

15.  Defending Against the Base Hit ...........................118

16.  Tactical Defense ...................................................127

17.  Defensive Signs and Pick-offs .............................129

18.  The Rundown ........................................................132


## PART   V

### Team Offense

19.  The Percentages ...................................................135

20.  The Sacrifice and Squeeze Bunts ..........................138

21.  The Hit-and-Run, Steal and Bunt-and-Run ............ 141

22.  Giving the Signs ...................................................143

23.  Coaching the Bases ..............................................146


## PART VI

### Team Organization and Development

24.  Matching Players with Positions ...........................148

25.  Practice Sessions ................................................. 154

# INTRODUCTION

Since World War II, there has been a tremendous change in the makeup and direction of "kid baseball", as it is called. Adults, showing an unprecedented interest in the activity, have initiated and developed programs in thousands of towns across the United States—programs that provide wholesome recreation for millions of youngsters and are often a source of pride and joy to the community in which they exist.

The young player of today is smartly uniformed and fully equipped. He plays on a miniature Big League diamond ruled by uniformed umpires. He often plays before large crowds and occasionally gets his name in a newspaper.

The professional recreation people say all this represents a commendable contrast to the pre-war kid baseballer who did most of his playing in a vacant lot, or cow pasture, with a ball that was more friction tape than ball. They add, however, that the diamond programs have mushroomed so rapidly that baseball "education"—the teaching of individual and team play—has, unwittingly to be sure, dragged behind.

Many leaders, of course, have had wide baseball experience and are well-equipped to teach the game. But many thousands who have eagerly rushed in to handle this vast new army of youngsters, are relatively inexperienced and seeking aid. Then, too, there are others—father, uncles and brothers of players—who would like to help out, but hesitate to do so because of an admitted lack of knowledge about baseball.

Since there has been a dearth of written material about the subject, it has been the objective of the writer to produce a manual that will provide player, manager, fan and father-coach with the kind of useful, practical information that can be applied to amateur baseball, especially to those programs for 8 to 18 year-olds.

Most of the book is devoted to individual and team play with these two major groupings broken down and presented in logical fashion and also in the order of importance. For example, the three major skills—batting, running and throwing—are given first. The specialized skills, such as pitching and catching, follow. Team play, of course, is divided in two parts—offense and defense.

The reader will find diagrams and sketches supplementing the words that describe the more important and complicated parts of play. He will also discover that the text is sprinkled with many of the colorful phrases used by the professionals, such as "throw wild to the glove side", "stand on your big toes", and "show the button". The pros have used these expressions for years because they so aptly describe important points about diamond play.

It should be pointed out that the fundamentals of baseball—batting, fielding, throwing, running the bases—are as basic for the Little Leaguer as they are for the professional playing in the Big Leagues. As a result, there is something in the following text for every baseball enthusiast.

PART I
THE BASIC SKILLS

Chapter 1

# Batting and Bunting

Batting, or "putting the wood to the ball", is the key to the success or failure of the ball club and the individual.

There is no great mystery about what makes a boy a good hitter. He has to have:

1. A certain amount of natural ability
2. A mastery of the fundamentals
3. Confidence in his ability to hit

The phrase "natural ability" covers a great deal. It means strong arms, wrists and hands; quick reflexes, good coordination, perfect eyesight and speed afoot.

Regardless of how much natural ability a boy has, however, he won't hit as well as he should if he doesn't master the fundamentals and believe in his ability to hit the ball as it comes through the strike zone. Self-confidence, of course, stems from success. And success in batting comes from practice. The following text describes the mechanics of hitting as they apply to ball players in general. By following the principles involved, the well-coordinated boy could easily become the batting star of his team; the average boy could certainly become a better-than-average hitter.

## The Stance

If a boy is right-handed, he should turn his left side to the pitcher; the right side if left-handed.

The body should be fairly erect and relaxed with the

weight distributed evenly on both feet. The hips and shoulders should be level. The feet should be shoulder-width apart with the toe of the front foot even with the instep of the rear foot. When the ball is being delivered, the batter's heels should be up slightly, his knees flexed slightly. A most apt phrase is—"stand on the big toes!"

## The Stride

As the ball is being delivered to the plate, the batter should raise his front foot just above the ground and slide

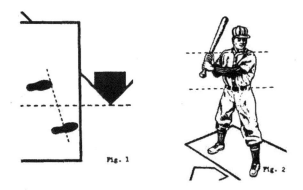

Fig. 1          Fig. 2

**As indicated at left, batter's body should face pitcher slightly, with toe of front foot about in line with instep of rear foot. Middle of body should also be about opposite tail end of plate. Batter's hips and shoulders should always be level, as shown in sketch at right.**

it forward (toward pitcher) about six inches. This step, a critical part of hitting, begins what is generally termed "timing". All other movements that are a part of batting flow from it.

To learn and practice The Stride, beginners should first take the stance just described and place hands on hips. Then, simply step forward. And back. Forward. And back. Forward. And back.

Now, well begin to build on the timing cycle. As the front foot comes down, the batter is to rotate the trunk toward the pitcher. From the hips up, he twists the body sharply and as far as it will go.

Again stand with the feet shoulder-width apart, toe of front even with instep of back foot. Place hands on hips. "Stand on the big toes."

Ready? Step-and-twist. Back to starting position.

Again . . . step-and-twist. Back.

Step-and-twist. Back

### Arm and Hand Positions

Let's try now to add the arm movements to The Stance and then coordinate them with The Stride.

Right-handed batters: place your left palm against the front of your right shoulder, little finger down, thumb up. Move the left hand forward about six inches and make a fist.

Left-handed batters: place your right palm against the front of your left shoulder, little finger down, thumb up. Move the right hand forward about six inches and make a fist.

The elbow of the arm that is now extended across the body should have almost no bend in it and there should be no strain on the arm. This is the arm and hand that guide the bat through the swing. The opposite arm and hand provide the power.

Make a fist with the Power Hand and place it on *top* of the Guiding Hand.

Raise the elbow of the Power Arm so it is level with the top of the shoulder. There will be some strain there. Drop this elbow slowly until there is no strain. (The elbow of the Power Arm should come to a stop about two inches below the top of the shoulder.)

Keep elbows and hands away from the body!

## The Swing

Now you're ready to start the Swing. Try it as follows:

Assume the Batting Stance with arms and hands in proper position.

Move both hands slowly away from the body until the arms are fully extended in front of the Power Shoulder. Bend both wrists down as far as they will go. Move the arms slowly toward the imaginary pitch. As the hands come in front of the Guiding Shoulder, stop. That's about where the bat will make contact with the ball. Once that contact is made, roll the wrists toward the pitcher as far as they will go and continue the swing, carrying the arms as far around the body as you can reach.

Practice the move slowly a few times, then increase the speed of the swing.

You should be ready now to work it into the foot and body movements.

## Hit Against The Front Foot

The hitter should start the swing a split second after the front foot strikes the ground. As the front foot digs in, the hips twist and the arms and hands snap the bat out and around. Without a bat, go smoothly from one movement to another. Make it one fluid surge of power. Here we go!

Take the Batting Stance.

Ready? Step. Twist-and-Swing. Back

Step. Twist-and-Swing. Back.

Step. Twist-and-Swing. Back.

Pick up a bat. Look for the label or trademark, and swing the bat slowly. As the bat goes over the plate, that trademark should *always* be straight up or facing the ground. If it isn't, you will be hitting against the grain of the wood and the bat is apt to split. Now, turn your hands so the middle knuckles are about in a straight line.

Again assume the batting stance. The big end of the bat should be pointing skyward and not laid back so it is horizontal. Without moving the feet, bring the bat through the swing, using the form you practiced before. As the bat gets
directly in front of the body, stop. Is the bat level with the
ground? If not, raise or lower the end and continue the swing. Try it again, with the stride, and KEEP THE BAT LEVEL WITH THE GROUND!

Start the cycle once more and check yourself.

Stance—Are hands and feet in proper position? Are hips and shoulders level? Is the body fairly erect and relaxed?
Is it balanced on the big toes?

Step-Twist-Swing—Was the label of the bat up as it went across the plate? Was the swing level with the ground? Were the arms fully extended. Did you roll your wrists? Did you go all the way around—"follow through"?

Once the batter learns the proper form, he is ready to step to the plate and face a pitcher.

**In the Batter s Box**

Generally speaking, the back end of the plate should be about even with the middle of the hitter's body. The big end of the bat should extend to one or two inches beyond the outside edge of the plate when the arms are fully extended.

The type of pitcher and the situation tells the batter how to adjust. If the pitcher is very fast and relies on his fast ball most of the time, the batter should stand as far back as possible. If the pitcher uses a curve most of the time, the batter ought to move to the front of the box and try to hit the curve before it breaks. If a runner is on base and the "Steal" sign is flashed, the batter should stand back as far as he can so the catcher will be forced back a few steps, adding to the length of his throw. If the count is 3 balls and no strikes, the batter should crowd the plate and make as tough a target as he can for the pitcher.

## Hit It Where It's Pitched!

Once the pitcher starts his move, the batter wants to stand absolutely still, but relaxed, never taking his eyes off the pitcher. He concentrates most when the pitcher is about to release the ball. It's not a good practice to try to follow the ball all through the pitcher's windup. As the ball comes whistling toward the plate, the batter must get into the habit of watching it all the way—until it actually meets the bat. He must not pull his head away from the plate until *after* the ball has been hit.

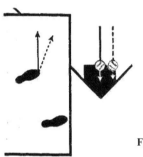

Batter should adjust forward step to hit ball where it's pitched.

Fig. 3

The batter must start the weight forward early! Take your stride as the pitcher's striding foot hits the ground.

*Starting* the forward stride and striding in the right direction are equally important. Always step toward the ball, but move so that the ball will arrive near the "meat end" of the bat.

For example: If the pitch comes directly over the center of the plate, the hitter can step along a line parallel to one running between the pitcher and the plate. (He has already made certain, with his practice swing, that the heavy end of the bat would come over the heart of the plate). If the ball is wide, he should adjust the direction of his step accordingly. He cannot possibly hit the ball well if he steps the same way on an inside and outside pitch—he must adjust the step.

In addition, he must adjust the level of his swing if the ball is low. If the batter holds his hands in the position advocated here—just below the level of the Power Shoulder —he need only adjust the hands for pitches in the strike zone that are above the belt line. Below the belt line, he should bend his knees so that the bat still remains level with the ground as it goes around.

Except when trying to place-hit, always hit the ball in *front,* or to the pitcher's side of the plate.

Now, we come to the problem of *where* to hit the ball. Ball players talk a great deal about "pulling" the ball and "hitting to right", or "hitting to left". The best slogan for a young hitter to adopt is this one: "hit the ball where it is pitched." That means this to a right hand hitter (the opposite to a left-hander): If the ball is "outside", hit directly into right field. If it's inside, hit into left field. If it's over the center of the plate, hit into center field. By doing this you can hit with full power and have a better chance of getting solid wood on the ball. You also keep the defense from "ganging" up on you. A boy who always hits to the same field is not as valuable to his team as the boy who hits to *all* fields.

This matter of hitting the ball where it is pitched applies to the curve as well as the fast ball. As a matter of fact, it's probably more important to follow this practice when batting against a curve-ball pitcher. A curve to a right hand hitter is normally going down and to the outside. The hitter *might* be able to hit the ball if he strides straight ahead, but most of the time the end of the bat will be pulling *away* from the ball.

A right hand hitter should hit the outside curve ball into right field—just as he would the outside pitch; the left hand hitter should try to whack it into left.

### Aim At The Hitting Lanes

The batter's constant objective is to "hit the ball where they ain't, which is a crude way of saying: hit between the fielders. It will help the hitter if, when he stands at the plate, he tries to visualize the "hitting lanes". He should carry a mental picture of lines running from the plate to the outfield, but between the third baseman and 3rd base; between the third baseman and the shortstop; over 2nd base; between the second baseman and the first baseman and between the first baseman and 1st base. He should try to drive the ball down one of these lines, depending on where it is pitched. The hitting lanes give the batter five definite targets, instead of a single "blind" one.

### Don't Guess-Hit

This writer is a strong opponent of "guess hitting" for amateur players. The guess hitter tries to decide before the pitch is delivered whether it's going to be a fast ball or **a** curve. He also decides whether or not he will swing at the next pitch. Only an exceptionally talented hitter can do this successfully. The average hitter can't afford to be fooled, or **to** let **a** good pitch go by, which is just what he'll do every time he "guesses" wrong.

The best advice for any youngster is this:

Be ready to hit every pitch. Be ready to hit it to any field.

Always expect the fast ball and it will never fool you.

If the pitcher throws a curve, you have time to adjust your swing. You may at least get enough wood on the ball to foul it off, which gives you another chance.

Bunting

Bunting is essentially a part of hitting, but the technique is very different. In the old days, a well executed bunt gave the fans a thrill. Now, the home run is the great attraction. Nevertheless, the bunt is an important weapon for the team at bat. Players and managers alike realize this, of course, when it fails to work at a crucial point in the Big Game.

The bunt is used for two purposes—to advance a runner; to get the batter on base. Since each bunt has a different objective, each is executed differently.

The "sacrifice" bunt is used to put the ball *on the ground* out of reach of any fielder so that a runner, or runners, will have enough time to advance one or more bases.

Too often, youngsters think more about getting on base than putting the ball down. This reverses the intent of the "sacrifice".

To sacrifice, the batter turns the feet and body so that he faces the pitcher squarely. Imagine, for the moment, that the hitter is right-handed. As the pitcher gets on the rubber, the batter takes his normal batting position. Just as the pitcher starts his throwing move, the batter turns left, stepping back and left with the left foot. He moves his right foot up to the spot vacated by the left. In two quick steps the feet should be parallel, with the toes pointing at the pitcher. The right foot should be even with the plate and just inside the batter's box.

To get the feeling of this particular skill, forget for the moment that a bat is to be used. Pretend, instead, that you are going to catch the pitched ball. If the ball were high, you might straighten up a bit. If low, you would squat slightly. You would also have your arms extended toward the pitcher with your hands where you could see them, following the flight of the ball.

Follow the same principle when using a bat.

## Catch It With The Bat

Before going any further with the act of bunting, let's turn our attention to the bat grip. If you are a right hand batter, make a fist with the right hand, with the little finger facing the ground. Extend the index finger and raise the thumb. Now crook the index finger as though you would pull the trigger of a gun. Put the bat between thumb and forefinger at a point some two to four inches above the label and squeeze hard. (Be sure the flesh doesn't extend over the hitting surface.) The V formed in back of the bat between thumb and forefinger acts as a cushion and will absorb the shock of the ball hitting the bat.

Wrap the left hand very loosely around the bat just under the knob (palm down). Extend the arms forward. Keep the bat level with the ground and "catch" the ball with the meat end, which should be extended into the strike zone.

To place the ball toward 1st, keep the right hand rigid, push the left hand forward. To bunt to 3rd, keep the right

To sacrifice, bunter faces pitcher, catches ball on meat end of bat.

Fig. 4

hand rigid, pull the left hand back. But always "catch" the

ball as though you had a glove *on—don t poke or jab at **it**.* (Opposite applies for left hand hitters.)

## Bunt The Strike!

When a batter is ordered to sacrifice, he never tries to lay down a bad pitch. If, after turning to the bunting position, the pitch looks like a ball, the hitter should deliberately yank the heavy end of the bat back. This helps convince an uncertain umpire, aids the runner and avoids the possibility of a foul tip.

A batter should always anticipate a sign for the sacrifice when a runner is on 1st, 1st and 2nd with none out and the score close. All of the circumstances involved are described in more detail in Chapter 20.

## Bunting For The Hit

The right and left hand batter move differently when bunting to get on base but both need the element of surprise to be successful. The right-hander, at the last possible moment, draws back his right foot and puts his weight **on** it. At the same time, he brings both hands diagonally down and to the left until they are in front of the left hip. He then pulls the left hand back, letting the bat slide through the right until just before it reaches the label.

The bat is now level with the ground with the end extending into the strike zone. The left hand is close to the left hip, but above and in back of it. The right hand is about eight inches in front and above the left hip.

The batter is now in position to "chase" the ball. He pushes off the back foot and goes after it with the left foot leading. The ball should make contact with the bat at just about the time the left foot strikes the ground. The batter then keeps going for 1st base.

To reconstruct:

The pitcher's arm is coming down. Just before the ball reaches the plate, the batter rocks back on his right foot, drops the bat, steps toward it with the left foot, bunts and keeps going.

If the ball is wide, he faces the bat toward 1st and, in a sense, tries to keep contact with it as he runs toward 1st.

If it's an inside pitch, he makes his step toward 3rd to bunt the ball.

The left hand batter, also striving for surprise, brings the bat down and takes his step with a single motion. The right hand drops to a point just above the right hip; the bat slides through the left until just before it reaches the label. The first step is also made with the back foot—but it's a cross over-step as the body pivots right. The left foot crosses in *front* of the right and toward 1st base if the pitch is inside, toward the mound if outside. After the ball *is* bunted, of course, the batter keeps running.

As the left hand batter gets more proficient with the "drag" bunt, he can start concentrating on just where to place it. He should try to put the ball at the first baseman's extreme right and the pitcher's extreme left in the bunting area. If he can force the first baseman, or even the second baseman, to field the ball in this area, he has a base hit. If the first baseman ignores the bunt, it will take both the second baseman and pitcher too long to get to the ball to make the put-out. If the first baseman fields the ball, the second baseman or pitcher will have to cover 1st base, which will be very difficult.

One more thought: The batter should remember that he doesn't have to bunt the ball. Actually, he should bunt the pitch he likes best. Many right hand bunters like the ball low and outside. Left hand batters usually like the inside pitch between the waist and the shoulders.

Chapter 2

# Fielding and Throwing

Each position has its own peculiar requirements. The first baseman has to learn things no other player need bother about. Ditto the shortstop, catcher, pitcher, or outfielder.

There are a number of points about catching and throwing the ball, however, that apply to all players. A fielder, for example, should always try to use both hands when making a catch. The hands should "give" and be "soft" when the ball strikes them. If the ball is being received above the waist, the thumbs should be together with the palms facing the ball, fingers spread and pointing skyward. If below the waist, the little fingers are to be together with the fingers pointing to the ground. Whenever possible, the ball should be caught at shoulder-height, so that the fielder can throw without loss of motion.

Proper movement of the hands, however, represents only one part of the fielding technique. To make a good, clean catch a player must get *to* the ball and, if possible, receive it in front of the body at a point that is in line with the middle of the body. This means the fielder *must move his feet!*

On balls that are not very wide of a player's position, the "boxer's" step can be used. This involves shifting one foot to the side and closing with the other so that when the ball is received, the feet are at the width they were before the ball was hit or thrown. It's quick step right, close left, step right; or step left, close right, step left.

On balls hit very wide, however, the player should make his first move a "cross-over" step. Try this experiment:

With the feet a little more than shoulder-width apart, assume that a ball is hit wide to your left. Take a step with the left foot. You really haven't moved very much, have you? Take the original position again. This time, throw all your weight left, pivot left on the balls of both feet and step out with the right foot. You have not only covered ground, but you are in good position to race to the ball. Try it to the right.

Infielders and outfielders can start working on the cross-over and boxer's step in the gym, long before the season starts. This simple drill will help:

Players pair off and face each other with about 10 feet between them. They roll a ball to each other, first to one side, then the other.

## Watch The Hitter

As the pitcher takes his windup to deliver the ball to the plate, the fielder's eyes should be on the batter.

Prior to the pitcher's move, the fielders should be relaxed with the body bent forward at the waist, hands resting on the knees. As the ball reaches the plate, the fielder should take a short forward step and straighten the body. If the batter hits the ball, each fielder is moving and no matter where the ball goes, the defense has a "jump" on it.

Here are the major points involved in fielding ground balls:

1. Prior to the pitch, be sure the weight of the body is distributed evenly on both feet.

2. Get the heels off the ground as the ball reaches the plate and take a short forward step,

3. Be aggressive. "Play the ball, don't let the ball play you," is a good axiom to remember.

4. Move so that the ball can be fielded well in front of the body and in the middle of the body.

5. Keep the hands low.

6. Try to catch the ball just as it leaves the ground or at the top of the bounce.

7. When receiving the ball, have the feet parallel, but wide apart. Keep the tail down. If the tail is high, the player's feet are too close together, a common fault.

8. Watch the ball until it is in the glove and "catch it soft."

## "Show The Button"

For all-around fielding practice on ground balls, managers will find this to be a good outdoor drill:

Put a boy at normal infield depth. Put a second boy 20 feet behind him to back up. Off to the left of the fielder, at about 15 feet, place a third boy. Have a fourth boy stand next to the hitter, but also to the fielder's left, to feed balls to the hitter. Get six or a dozen baseballs and constantly hit to the right and left of the fielder. Have the fielder put his right hand in his back pocket and field the ball with glove only. And, still with the glove hand, instruct him to shovel the ball to the boy waiting at his left. This boy tosses to the one assisting the coach. After several hits to either side, the fielder takes the back-up position, the others rotate clockwise.

The coach wants to compliment when compliments are in order, correct defects when they appear. He should keep telling the fielder to "show the button of your cap . . . show the button of your cap." If the coach sees the button, which is right on top of the head, he can be sure that the fielder is watching the ball go in the glove. On the other hand, if he sees the letter just above the peak of the cap, he knows the boy has his head "up". "Don't show the letter," he should say. "Show that button!"

Boys enjoy this drill and it serves to develop the important habit of keeping the glove low and the eyes on the ball.

## Fly Chasing

When chasing a fly, fielders should try to get under the ball as quickly as possible and wait for it to descend. Amateur players shouldn't attempt to catch the fly ball on the run if it isn't necessary. Every player should get in the habit of adjusting the body to throwing position after every catch—whether during practice or a game.

(Some of the finer points about fly chasing are covered in Chapter 10.)

Throwing

Throwing, like batting, gives the beginner a good deal of trouble, despite the theory that boys throw "naturally." To get a youngster to start and continue throwing correctly, a manager might instruct him as follows:

**Before throw, wrist grid arm should be forced back as far as possible.**

Fig. 5

Fig. 6

Draw a line on the ground about three feet long, with one end pointed at the target. Straddle the line at the opposite end with the feet about six inches apart.

Raise the elbows sideward in relaxed fashion until they are at shoulder-height.

(Following movements are for right hand throwers, opposite for left.)

Twist the body right, take a normal step forward with the left foot, bringing it down to the left of the line.

As the left foot strikes the ground, sharply twist hips and shoulders to the left.

Pick up right foot and bring it down near the left.

Return to the original position, then repeat several times.

To work in the movement of the throwing arm, the manager can add these instructions:

Raise the throwing elbow sideward to shoulder height. Raise the hand to a position directly above it, with palm facing target. Bend wrist and hand back as far as they will go. Pull the elbow back as far as it will go. Twist the body toward the throwing hand slightly.

Raise the left hand and elbow to shoulder height.

Now—start the step, stretch the left hand toward the target; bring the throwing arm forward, elbow leading. The elbow should be about opposite the throwing shoulder as the front foot hits the ground. As the striding foot hits, the upper torso twists left, the throwing hand snaps forward and down.

Put all the movements together and practice them until the throw becomes easy and rhythmic. If the ball does not strike the target at the right height, it is being released too soon, or too late.

# Chapter 3

# Running the Bases and Sliding

Of all the baseball skills, running the bases is the simplest to master. Yet, its teaching and practice is often sorely neglected among amateurs.

As with many other aspects of baseball, the situation that develops after the ball is hit tells the runner what to do. If, for example, he is trying to beat out an infield roller, the runner's only concern is to get *to* 1st ahead of the throw. If the ball goes through the infield for a single, the runner wants to make a turn at the base. If the batter drives a pitch over the outfielder's head for a sure double he uses one running pattern; if it's a triple, he uses another. And if it looks like an inside-the-park homer, he might use still a different pattern.

Here are the techniques involved, starting with the attempt to beat a throw to 1st.

As the right hand batter hits the ball, his weight is on his front foot. To get started to 1st, he should drive off that foot, taking the first step with the right.

The left-hand hitter's weight is also on his front foot. He can usually cross over with his left to start toward 1st.

Whether right or left-handed, the batter starts down the line like a sprinter leaving the starting blocks. He takes *one* look at the ball, then concentrates on running. His weight is well forward, body as low as he can get it. His first steps are short and choppy with the feet fairly wide apart. As the runner gets about one-third the way down the line, he starts to straighten up and lengthen stride. He's erect at the half-way point and driving with full power.

When 1st base looms ahead, our runner should pretend that the finish line to his race with the ball is 15 feet on the *other side* of the bag. He should run "through" 1st, stepping on the base with either foot as he goes across.

The runner must *avoid jumping* at the base. He can't go forward any faster by going up. He must not slide, either, unless someone is attempting to tag him.

After crossing the bag, the runner should make a *direct* return to it. If any move is made toward 2nd—even a head-bob—the opposition can make a play on the runner and he might be tagged off base and called "out." Some managers advocate turning to the right after crossing the bag so there won't be any misunderstanding about what the runner has in mind. This is not always considered a good practice, however, as a runner will lose steps if there's an opportunity to go to 2nd. The important thing to remember is this:

Don't make a move to 2nd base unless you're going there!

The batter who cracks out a base hit wants to stretch it if he can. He also wants to draw a throw to 1st base and take advantage of a possible error.

To save the most number of steps and be in a good position to advance, this runner approaches 1st as any other, until he gets to a point some 15 to 20 feet in front of the base. Here, he makes a small dip to the right so that when he hits the bag, he will be headed straight for 2nd and not right field.

There is much dispute about how a runner should touch the bases as he circles them. Many managers and coaches say the runner should put the inside foot on the inside corner of the base, pivot left and cross over with the right to continue to the next base. Others say that in order to do this, the runner often has to break his stride. The best method, according to these managers, is for the boy to strike the bag with whichever foot comes up when he gets there.

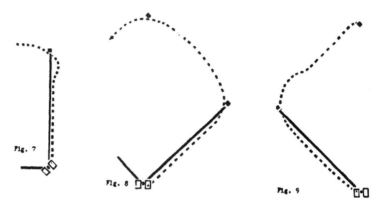

**From left to right are running patterns for bluff to 2nd, or two-base hit; a triple, scoring run from second. Note that the dip to right is only used in Figs. 7 & 9.**

Whichever method is used, there is one thing that *is* more important than any other, for sure: *touch the base!* If you miss it, go back!

On two-base hits, the batter makes his turn at 1st just as he does for a single—with a small dip to the right. On a triple—a ball the batter knows is going to be a triple—the dip at 1st is ignored.

If, after leaving 2nd, a runner intends to round 3rd, or continue to the plate, he should again make the little dip some 15 to 20 feet in front of the base.

When a runner, however, is trying for an inside-the-park home run, he should run the bases in a tight circle, pivoting as much as he can at every base.

As a general rule, a base runner is "on his own" when the

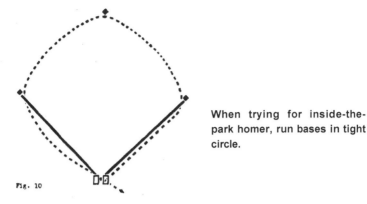

When trying for inside-the-park homer, run bases in tight circle.

Fig. 10

ball is in front of him. In other words, he—and not the coach—judges whether an attempt to advance should be made. Once the ball is in back of a runner, however, he should rely *entirely* on the instruction of the base coach. If a batter hits a ball into the right field corner, for example, he should look at the 3rd base coach as he approaches 2nd base and again as he leaves it. He should not look back at the ball!

Above all, a player should be taught to *run hard* and *keep running* until he either arrives safely at a base, or has clearly been put out. Don't forget, too, that a batter has an opportunity to run when:

1. The catcher drops a third strike.

2. "Ball Four" goes through the catcher. The ball is "in play" and, theoretically at least, the batter could circle the bases and score.

### Sliding

Many young ball players hesitate to learn to slide because they are fearful of being hurt. Actually, the boy who slides correctly has learned a skill that helps *prevent* injury.

There are two ways to slide—head first and feet first.

When a runner dives toward a base on his stomach, he goes straight in, or to one side and reaches for the base with a hand. It's not too difficult a slide, but it's hard on the stomach and not too efficient, except when used to avoid being picked off base by a pitcher.

Sliding feet first, on the other hand, takes a little practice and is a necessary skill for the ball player—amateur or professional. There are two basic methods.

1. The Hook Slide (or "fadeaway").

This is the most popular and probably the most useful. The body goes well to the side of the base as one toe reaches for a corner, making a small target for the infielder's tag.

2. The Leg-under, or Bent-leg Slide.

This slide is used mostly when a runner wants to go "straight in" to a base. It also enables the runner to come quickly to his feet in the event the ball eludes the defense.

It's best for players to learn how to slide as soon as possible, for the earlier the years, the lighter and more supple the body. Most boys, if they wait too long to start sliding, will find that they can only slide on one side, which is a disadvantage.

To get the proper form for the Hook Slide, sit down with legs extended. Turn to the right so all the weight is on the right hip. Bend the left leg so that the calf is at right angles to the thigh.

The toe of that foot *is* the "hooking" foot.

Now then, raise the hands over the head and lower the trunk until the back touches the ground. Swing the right foot to the right slightly and raise it a few inches. There you have it—a Hook Slide to the right.

Try it on the other side, reaching for the corner of the bag with the toe of the right foot.

When making the Hook Slide, remember to:
Spread the weight out as much as possible—get the back down.

Keep the outside foot (the one that's not hooking the bag) off the ground! If you don't, the spikes are apt to catch in the dirt. The weight of the body sliding forward will then turn the ankle down and out, causing a severe sprain, or break.

When making any slide, don't jump at the base! S-1-i-d-e up to it.

Keep your hands up, too. If your hands strike the ground, you might tear the flesh or get a bad wrist sprain. If you have trouble keeping your hands high, by the way, pick up dirt in each hand when you get on base and hang on to it.

To get the form for the "Leg-under" slide, sit down again with the legs stretched out in front. Double the right leg under the left, so that the right shin faces the "base". Roll over on your right hip slightly. Raise the hands over the head.

If the play is going to be close and you plan to go straight into the base, get your back down and reach for the base with the left toe. (Opposite for opposite side.)

If you want to stop at the base, or intend to continue on, ride in on the bent leg until it touches the base. Let the top foot go over the base; bring it down on the other side and with a little upward surge of the body, you'll be on your feet again and ready to continue. (Some runners like to bring top foot down on middle of base.)

To get a better idea of what we're talking about, sit in the bent-leg position. Ask someone to grab one of your hands and pull you forward. You come naturally to your feet, as you will see.

Sketch at left shows a hook slide. Note that right foot is clear of ground; that hands are up; that left toe touches corner of bag. Other sketch illustrates bent-leg slide.

### "Don't Be A Woman!"

There's one absolute rule about sliding. The boy who forgets it is going to get hurt. If you're going to slide, slide. Don't start to slide then decide to stand up. As the saying goes—don't be a woman and change your mind.

If a play is being made on you at 2nd or 3rd, always slide. If you over-run the bag, you'll be tagged out. If you slow up so you won't over-run the bag, you'll also be tagged out. you can over-run home plate, of course. But don't try to go in standing up unless you have the throw clearly beaten and the catcher is obviously not going to try to tag you. When in doubt, *always* slide.

Boys who can only slide on the right (or left) side, should use a hand to tag the base. If, for instance, you are going into 2nd base to beat a throw from left field, the second baseman will leave the left side of the base open. If you can only slide on your right side, do so. But go to the 3rd base side of 2nd and grab the base with your right hand as you go by.

There are two places a boy can practice sliding—at the beach, or in a jumping pit used for track and field events. In either case, boys must avoid jumping at the base, a habit they can form easily in the pit or at the seashore.

## PART II
## INDIVIDUAL DEFENSE

# Chapter 4

# Pitching

The value of the pitcher cannot be overestimated. He is not only the most important cog in the defense of any baseball team, he is also the life and spirit of the ball club. A strong, competent, confident pitcher can carry a weak team a long way—especially in the lower age groups. Weak pitching, on the other hand, will often keep an otherwise sound team in last place. If a boy has the potential, gets the proper instruction and works hard, the results can be mighty rewarding.

The pitcher should have the strongest throwing arm on the team. He also needs a sturdy body because, with the exception of the catcher, he works harder than any other player.

Above all else, however, a pitcher must be able to throw accurately. If a boy can't get the ball over the plate, in the strike zone, he had better give up pitching. With beginners, accuracy is almost as important as power. Here's why:

On a pitched ball, the batter can (a) swing and miss; (b) ground out to the infield; (c) hit a fly ball for an out; (d) foul out, or (e) get a base hit.

The odds are heavily in favor of the pitcher—*IF* he can keep the ball in the strike zone!

Thus, the manager of a team of youngsters might take this view:

"If I have a pitcher with superior control and a better than average arm—enough power to keep the batters from digging in and hitting at will—I have a boy who's definitely **a** member of the pitching staff."

## H-H-A

As indicated earlier, the pitcher needs something more than physical ability. He needs to be calmly aggressive, coolly efficient and possessed of good judgement. Most of all, he needs a fighting heart!

The pitcher must learn that no matter what his mates do, no matter what the score, or the inning, he's to always give his best. He ought to learn, too, that it's wise to keep his thoughts to himself—about the errors his teammates have made, about the walks he's given up, or the taunts of the fans or players on the opposing team. He should constantly say to himself:

"I've got three things to do—throw the ball over the plate, field my position, back up the bases."

In selecting a pitcher, the manager should look for "Head, Heart and Arm!"

## Skills Involved

Pitchers employ four different deliveries—underhand, side-arm, three-quarter and overhand. If **a** pitcher uses the underhand delivery, his throwing hand releases the ball below the belt line; if sidearm, from shoulder height; if overhand, above the head, and if three-quarter, halfway between the sidearm and overhand deliveries.

The pitcher should choose the delivery that is most *natural* —the one that gives him the greatest power and accuracy. Once he's made the choice, he should stick to it for a reasonable length of time and not try to throw underhand one day, overhand the next. Unnecessary experiments can injure the pitching arm permanently!

Regardless of whether a pitcher uses a sidearm or over-hand delivery, there are a number of fundamentals to be learned. Let's start with the wrist action. Good wrist action does a lot for a pitcher—it gives that extra "zing" to his fast ball and it gives him the good curve.

To get some idea of how to use the wrist, raise the pitching elbow to the level of the shoulder. Raise the pitching hand so it is directly above the elbow. Bend the wrist back as far as possible. Snap it forward. Repeat three or four times. Can you feel the muscles in the wrist and forearm area pull?

Fig. 13

**As pitcher brings hands overhead during full windup (left), back of glove and palm of throwing hand faces batter. When delivering ball, pitcher has 4 spots to pitch to (right), whether throwing fast ball or curve.**

With the body erect and facing the target, put your arm and hand again in throwing position. Lay the wrist back as far as you can. Move the elbow back as far as you can—until you feel muscle pulls all across the chest.

Now, start the arm forward, elbow leading. As the elbow conies opposite the shoulder, move the forearm forward and down; then snap the wrist down. Repeat several times without the ball. Then, put a ball in the pitching hand and without moving the feet see how far you can throw it.

### The Grip and Hand Action

Until a boy gets out of high school, he doesn't need to develop more than two basic pitches—the curve and the fast ball. In the first place, he'll get four pitches with the fast ball alone—low inside, low outside, high inside, high outside. Ditto the curve. If he then learns to change the speed of each pitch, he can double his assortment.

The overall grip is the same for the curve and fast ball; forefinger and middle finger spread in a comfortable V on top of the ball, thumb underneath.

For the fast ball from the overhand or three-quarter de-

Fig. 15                Fig. 16

**Pitchers usually run top fingers across figure 8 pattern when throwing fast ball and along stitches when throwing curve.**

livery, the hand should be directly behind the ball. When the ball leaves the hand it should rotate upward, or toward the pitcher. To make this spin more effective, pitchers usually grip the ball across the stitches—some across the fat part of the figure 8 pattern, some at the narrow part.

To throw the curve, the pitcher makes the ball spin, or rotate, away from the hitter at an angle. He wants the ball to go out and down; not on a horizontal plane or "flat."

To accomplish this, run the top fingers *along* the stitches. Go slowly through the delivery as with the fast ball. At the forward snap of the wrist, twist the hand outward and bear down on the outside finger. Beginners should first learn to twirl the ball at the proper angle. (It's a good idea to paint a large black spot on one side of the ball to help get the correct angle to the spin.)

To improve a pitcher's control, managers might consider erecting a set of "strings". Here's how it's done: Stretch a string between two poles, or trees at average shoulder height. Stretch out another one at knee height. Then tie two pieces of twine, 12" apart, to the top string and loop both around the bottom string. The rectangle forms the strike zone. To complete the job, build a pitching mound in front of the strings at the proper distance.

## The Windup

Let's switch to the body movements now, using the three-quarter delivery as our example since it is the most popular.

Two basic positions are employed—the full windup and the "stretch". The full windup is used mostly when the bases are unoccupied. In professional ball, it is used when runners

Sketch at left shows proper position for right-hand pitcher's feet at start of windup. Second sketch shows position at start of "stretch".

Fig. 17

Fig. 18

are on 3rd, on 2nd and 3rd, or on 1st, 2nd and 3rd. Pitchers usually "stretch" with runners on 1st, or 1st and 2nd, and also 1st and 3rd. The eight-year-old probably should first be taught to throw from the stretch position and then gradually be introduced to the full windup.

Before starting any move, the pitcher must learn how and where to stand on the mound. The rules say he must have one foot in contact with the pitching rubber until the ball is delivered. This means his pitching foot—the right foot for a right hander, the left for a southpaw—is to be an the plate at the start of windup and remain in contact until the body is in the final part of the delivery cycle. (The pitcher cannot step forward to the pitching plate and make that part of the windup.) The toe of the pitching foot ought to extend over the forward edge of the rubber with the heel on top. The weight should be on the back foot, located comfortably behind the rubber. The pitching hand holds the ball out of the batter's sight behind the pitching leg. As soon as the pitcher gets his eyes on the target, with the catcher in proper receiving position, he can start his move.

Here's a step-by-step explanation of how it's done by a right hander:

Shift the weight forward to the right foot and bend the body forward slightly, at the same time extend the hands backward. Straighten the trunk, swing the hands forward and bring them together in front of the chest.

Shift the weight to the back foot and at the same time carry the hands up until they are just above the peak of the cap.

At this point arch the back as much as possible.

Twist the pitching foot to the right, but keep contact with the plate.

Pivot the body right, swing the left leg forward, start the hands down.

As the hands reach a point just below the right shoulder, separate them, drawing the throwing arm back, moving the glove hand forward. As the hands part, start the big stride toward the plate, "kicking" away from the pitching rubber.

When the front foot strikes the ground, throw

Sweep the right hand down and across the body.

Bring the right foot up so it's even with the left.

To drill several pitchers, the manager can line them up side by side facing an imaginary catcher. Each move can then be taught simultaneously.

Once the pitcher has mastered the windup, he can start thinking about pointers like these:

1. As the hands come together in front of the chest, the palm of the throwing hand should face the batter. The full back of the glove hand should face the batter. This way, the ball cannot be seen. If the back of the glove faces 1st and the back of the throwing hand 3rd, enough of the ball and throwing hand can be seen to tell the batter whether a fast ball or curve is coming.

2. Fix the grip as the hands reach the top of their upward swing.

3. Imagine there is a line from the toe of the pitching foot to the plate. If the pitcher is a right hander, his left foot should come down to the left of that line; to the right if he's left-handed. If he doesn't do this, the pitcher will be throwing across the body, or against the natural movement of the body.

4. Always pitch from the same spot on the rubber if control is good. If the ball is going to batter at right height, but off the plate, move the pitching foot to a different spot on the rubber.

All movements, by the way, should be natural and rhythmic.

### The Stretch Move

The so-called "stretch" move is used with runners on base. It enables the pitcher to hold runners close to the base before the pitch and also gives him a chance to pick off runners who[1] take too long a lead.

A right-hander should stand with his left foot in front of the rubber, his right foot on it and his life side facing the plate. (Opposite for left-handers.) The feet should be about shoulder-width apart with the weight distributed evenly and comfortably. The toe of the left foot is usually in line with the heel of the right foot.

At the start of the move, the hands are lifted above the head, brought together as they start downward to a spot in front of the chest. The arms are kept away from the body and not brought to rest against it.

Just before the pitch, the hands must be brought to a complete stop, (usually at chest level) otherwise the pitcher can be charged with a balk.

To throw to the plate, the pitcher momentarily shifts his weight to the rear foot, quickly lifts the front foot and strides toward the plate. The right foot is brought up even with the left after the ball is released.

### Pick-Off Moves

Some of the leagues for the youngest boys—Little League for example—do not permit leading away from the bases, so attempts to catch a runner off base by a throw from the pitching plate are not necessary. Once a boy reaches the age of 11 or 12, however, it's time he learned this important pitching requirement.

Here's how to begin:

Take the "stretch" position, holding the hands in front of the chest. Under the rules, only one part of the body can now be moved, unless the pitcher is in the act of throwing to a base or the plate. That little piece of anatomy is the head. If a pitcher learns to use his head with runners on base—and no joke intended—he can help himself a great deal.

Right-handers, first of all, look over their left shoulders to see the 1st base runner; past the right shoulder to see the 2nd base runner and straight ahead for the 3rd base runner. (Opposite for the left-hander.)

The most difficult move for the right-hander, of course, is

toward 1st. After taking the stretch, the pitcher should always make one or two moves of the head before throwing to the plate. He can drop his chin, turn his head slowly toward 1st, slowly away, quickly back to first, then pitch! The object of the head move here is to drive the runner back toward 1st—or at least get him leaning toward 1st—just before the pitch. If the pitcher decides to throw the ball to 1st, he wants to make a head move that will encourage a runner to stretch the lead.

After a pitcher has practiced the "head bob" awhile, he then must learn to coordinate it with his feet. Base runners usually steal bases because of the weakness of the pitcher and not, as generally believed, because of a defect in the catcher's play. And, if the pitcher does everything else right, the runner steals on the pitcher's feet. In other words, the pitcher's feet tell the runner whether to break for the next base, stay put, or get back to the base he's leading away from. It follows then, that the pitcher must be careful of how he moves the two feet. As discussed on page , the runner breaks for the next base when the pitcher's front foot comes up and starts toward the plate. The longer it takes that foot to come down, the longer it takes to release

**The "jump" move to 1st.**

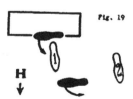

Fig. 19

H

the ball and the more "jump" the runner gets. Thus, when delivering the ball to the plate the pitcher should take the forward stride as quickly as possible. (A high kick with the striding foot is a common fault.)

The right-hander uses two different foot moves to make the throw to 1st. Some managers teach the "jump" move, others say a pivot is better. It has been the experience of this writer that the "jump** move is better for the average-sized or under-sized pitcher, while the pivot is easier for pitchers with very long legs.

To learn the jump move, do this: Take the stretch position. Pick up the right foot and turn it as far to the left as possible. Plant it. Swing the body left, step toward 1st with the left foot and throw.

Try it a little faster this way: Shift the weight to the front foot. Hop to the right foot as the right foot is twisting left; with all the weight on the right foot, step toward 1st with the left and throw. With a little practice, you'll be amazed at how fast you can get the ball to 1st.

To make the "pivot" move, simply take the stretch position with the right foot twisted as far left as is comfortable. The pitcher now either steps directly toward the plate, or directly toward 1st to throw. This move is somewhat slower than the "jump" move, but the right heel stays still. Every pitcher who uses the jump move gives advance warning with the right heel, as mentioned on page

It doesn't make any difference, however, which of these two moves the pitcher chooses, he still has to learn one more thing—when to throw. He should always try to throw when the runner is moving *away,* or leaning away, from the base. The runner usually begins to lead away as the pitcher raises his hands to start the stretch. It's a good idea then to learn to make the jump or pivot move to first with the hands in three different positions—from the very top of the stretch, half way down and from the stop position.

The left-hander, obviously, has a great advantage in holding runners on 1st. He's looking directly at the runner and that alone will make the runner cautious. With a runner on 1st, the lefty should have the toe of his pitching foot about even with the instep of his right. He should practice the head-bob and the same trick of throwing from the three different stretch positions. His best move, however, is this:

He takes the stretch. He looks at the runner. He looks at the plate. He turns his head back to the runner. And—just as he starts to turn the head to the plate again, he steps toward 1st. If the lefty works hard on this move, he'll pick more runners off 1st than he ever dreamed possible.

On throws to 2nd base, all pitchers should use the "jump" move, turning in the direction of the glove hand. (A right-hander would turn left, for example.) If the runner is safely back, or if the shortstop or second baseman fail to cover, don't throw the ball. (No balk on feint to 2nd.)

One more thing: If the pitcher is standing on the mound and suddenly sees the runner break, he should "back-off*— take his pitching foot off the rubber, and move it toward 2nd base. When a runner is stranded between the bases, the pitcher (or any fielder) should charge the runner, favoring the base *ahead* of the runner.

With runners on 3rd base, the pitcher may use either the stretch or full windup. If he uses the full windup, he should shorten the arm swing and quicken the move. He must *never* pump more than once!

## The Fielding Pitcher

Pitchers and managers should pay a great deal of attention to the techniques of fielding the ball around the mound. After the ball leaves his hands, the pitcher becomes an infielder. Like the other infielders, he has a spot to go to on every play.

The hardest thing for a young pitcher to learn is to go to his left on *every* ball hit to his left and to start *immediately!* Very often, the batter will hit a sharp bouncer between the first and second basemen. Both will try for it. This leaves 1st base open. It's the pitcher's job to get to 1st ahead of the runner and take the throw if the ball is fielded. He can't possibly make it, however, unless he starts running to his left at the crack of the bat. If he's not going to be involved in the play, on the other hand, all he has to do is stop.

To cover the base, the pitcher runs as fast as he can for a spot near the foul line that is about 10 feet to the home plate side of 1st. When he gets near this spot, he turns left so he can run along the inside of the base line (not in the base line). After catching the ball, he looks down for the base, hits the 2nd base side of the sack with his right foot and springs toward 2nd, out of the way of the oncoming runner.

With runners already on base, the pitcher, after tagging 1st, should quickly face the infield to keep them from advancing.

The beginning pitcher has a difficult time remembering that his feet should be parallel after delivering the ball to the plate. This will enable him to move right, left or straight ahead to field batted balls. It will also make it easier for him to knock down or catch those line drives that come right at him! Sometime a big pitcher has this trouble—his pitching foot comes down ahead of his striding foot. When this happens, the striding foot should quickly be brought up even with the pitching foot.

On a bunt with a runner on 1st, or on 3rd, the pitcher is responsible for everything in front of him that is out of reach of the catcher. With a runner on 2nd, he takes everything that is to his right of the imaginary line to the plate (first baseman takes everything on the left). These fielding areas are diagrammed on pages 115 and 116.

A swinging hit to the pitcher's box with a runner on 1st can get a pitcher in hot water if he always tries for the double play with less than two out. Unless it's a hard smash, the pitcher should ignore the runner going to 2nd and concentrate on putting out the batter. (He has little chance of getting the runner going to 2nd and if he misses he will have runners on 1st and 2nd with less than two out, instead of a runner on 2nd with an additional out in the score-book. )

Pitchers should let the other infielders handle pop-ups in the area of the mound, and think only about covering an open base if necessary.

## Backing Up The Bases

Getting off the mound to back up the bases is another important duty of the pitcher. As can be seen in Figs. 42-48, the pitcher backs up the third baseman on a single with a runner on 1st, the catcher on a single with a runner on 2nd, If both 1st and 2nd are occupied and the batter singles, the pitcher should hustle to a point off the left field foul line that is half way between 3rd and home. He can then back up 3rd or home, depending on where the play develops. But like going to his left on balls hit to his left, the pitcher must start *immediately.*

Any time a pitched ball gets by the catcher with runners on the bases, the pitcher should quickly cover home plate! In covering the plate, though, he ought to be careful of where he puts his feet. With his back to the runner, it would be foolhardy to stand in the basepath. It's best to leave one side of the base open, with the feet straddling the other and the body partly turned to the open side. If the ball is to the pitcher's right, he should leave the right corner open; if to the left, leave the left corner open.

## Beware the $1,000,000 Arm and 10¢ Head

A boy may have a strong arm and know all the mechanics of pitching, but if he doesn't think about the hitter's weak-nesses and strengths, he'll become nothing more than a "thrower" and will not help his team much.

A pitcher, even more than a catcher or manager, will know which of his deliveries the batter can or cannot hit. That is, if he studies the hitter constantly. This is just as true in Little League ball as it is in the Major Leagues. As a matter of fact, the younger the hitters are, the more faults they have. Thus, the young pitcher has a great advantage if he *thinks* about the hitters. Here are some general principles to follow:

1. Try to get "ahead" of the batter with the first pitch. That doesn't mean to groove the ball waist high and over the center of the dish. That means get the ball in the strike zone where you think the batter is weakest. If the batter stands so far away from the plate that his bat will not reach the outside corner, there is only one thing to do—pour that fast ball over the outside! If the hitter crowds the plate, fire it over his fists! Now then, if he looks strong at the plate and you know nothing about him, your best pitch is always low and outside or high and inside. Once around the league, the average pitcher should know *something* about the hitters. Don't worry about not learning all there is to know about *every* hitter. If you find one or two with weaknesses and can get them out consistently, you've made a good start.

2. The "situation" (as covered in Chapter 16) tells the pitcher a great deal about what to throw. If he expects a sacrifice, for example, he should pitch high, which will increase the possibility of a pop-up.

If a runner on 3rd streaks for home on a "suicide squeeze" play, he has to keep the ball away from the batter and put it where the catcher can make the tag. (Throwing at the feet of a right-handed batter is recommended; pitch-out if a lefty is at the plate.)

If the pitcher suspects a steal, he shouldn't throw a slow curve but stick to the fast ball.

3. When a pitcher has a 3-ball-2-strike count on a hitter, he should go to his best pitch. If his "best" is the curve, use the curve. It it's the fast ball, use the fast ball. Remember, though, that the "best pitch" may vary from game to game.

4. Try not to throw the same pitch twice in a row. Change speeds. Move the ball around the strike zone, always shooting at the corners. In doing this, your objective is to upset the hitter's timing. This is especially important when the pitcher faces the league's best hitters. The long foul, remember, is just another strike.

5. The pitcher who gets two quick strikes on the hitter should "waste" the next one by putting it where the batter can't possibly hit it.

6. Don't curve ball a weak hitter! Don't let up on a weak hitter! If the hitter is really weak, the fast ball can overpower him usually. If you throw the curve, you're throwing a slow speed pitch and it may be the only one this hitter can get his bat on.

7. If you're getting a hitter out regularly with one pitch, don't start experimenting with another.

8. If you're striking a lot of batters out and the game is going well for you, keep that pitching foot on the rubber and pitch as fast as the umpire will let you. On the other hand, if things are going bad, stall all you can to "cool off" the opposition.

**Chapter 5**

# Catching

A baseball team cannot function well without a good catcher. Strangely enough, not much effort is devoted to developing catchers among amateur players. If we were to guess why, we'd say this:

> The job doesn't appeal to youngsters starting out because it looks too complicated.

> It takes a lot of courage for beginners to get behind the bat.

> Managers, as a rule, don't know too much about catching.

Whatever the reasons, the catching spot should never be neglected. The fundamentals are not too difficult and as far as appeal is concerned—it's one of the most fascinating positions on the ball club. Once a boy has had a taste of catching it's hard to get him interested in playing any other position.

What kind of a boy makes a good catching prospect? A manager of an amateur team is rarely blessed with players who have "ideal" qualifications. He has to do the best with whatever material he has. When looking over his crop for a catcher, he knows he wants a boy with a strong arm, rugged body, courage and intelligence. Whether a boy has any great speed afoot, or whether he's big or small is not too important. The catcher, however, must have good hands and be able to move around behind the plate. (A heavy boy may not be able to run fast, but very often you will find him "light" on his feet. If he has the other qualifications mentioned, he's a catching prospect.)

**Shift Those Dogs!**

The more you study baseball, the more you will realize that the game is played as much with the feet as any other part of the body. This is particularly true of catching. The catcher simply *must* learn—and learn early—that he has to "shift the dogs.*' If he doesn't, he'll constantly drop third strikes, have pitched balls go through him and find runners stealing at will.

Even before a manager starts his catchers working with pitchers, he would do well to go over the basic steps very carefully. Then, as the boy begins to receive, the manager or coach can come back again and again to the fundamentals, until the player movers instinctively.

Let's begin with the easiest body and foot positions.

To start play, the catcher first squats down and flashes a "sign" to the pitcher. This sign, usually given with the bare hand, "tells" the pitcher what to throw.

To give the sign, the catcher draws his feet together and sits on his heels with knees pointing outward. The body is supported and balanced on the balls of the feet. The glove is hung over the end of the left knee with the little finger pointing down, the thumb up. The throwing hand is brought deep against the crotch to give the sign.

Once the sign is given, the catcher hops to the Receiving Position. His feet are now wide apart, his tail low. His glove hand makes the target. Some catchers put their bare hand behind the glove, some next to it, the others apart from it. This is optional. The bare hand, however, should be loose, with the thumb tucked under the other fingers.

The shifting of the body to get directly in front of the ball is the most difficult thing for catchers to learn. The youngster will be thinking only of getting his glove on the ball and he will do that by reaching, not by moving the feet.

On thrown balls to his right, the catcher should slide the right foot toward 1st base and closes with the left. On thrown balls to the left, it's slide left, close right.

When teaching the catcher these two steps, the coach or manager should toss the ball on one side then the other. Once the move seems to be mastered, it should be pointed out that it takes only % a second for a pitched ball to reach the plate. This means the slide-close to right and left must be done quickly and smoothly. It would be well then for

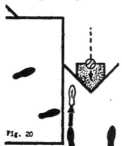

When pitch comes to center of catcher's body, he need only step forward with left foot to throw, as indicated left.

Fig. 20

the manager to back off about 60 feet and deliberately throw the ball to left and right of the catcher and to throw it fairly fast.

Shifting the feet enables the catcher to both catch the ball and throw. With runners on base, the proper shift becomes more important than ever.

Assume the batter is right-handed and the pitch is directly over the plate. What's the fastest foot-move one can make? Simple. Leave the right foot where it is in the Receiving Position, step forward left and throw.

Assume you have the same situation with the pitch going to the right, or "outside". Step right with the right foot. Instead of closing left, step diagonally right and forward with the left foot and throw.

On pitches that are "inside" to the right-handed hitter, step left for the catch and instead of closing right, step diagonally right with the right foot, plant it, step left and throw. It's to-the-left, to-the-right, forward-and-throw. If the pitch is far inside, causing the batter to jump back, a slight variation will help. Step left, bring the right foot left and plant it directly in back of the left, step forward with the left foot and throw. Use this step, too, if the runner is going from 2nd to 3rd, but throw in back of the batter if he's in the way.

For left hand hitters:

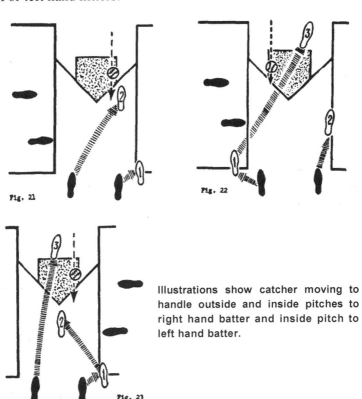

Fig. 21

Fig. 22

Fig. 23

Illustrations show catcher moving to handle outside and inside pitches to right hand batter and inside pitch to left hand batter.

On outside pitches—step left, bring the right foot in back of the left, plant it, step forward left and throw.

On inside pitches—step right, hop diagonally left and forward on the right foot, step forward left and throw.

If the catcher wants to throw to 1st with a left hand hitter at the dish, he can throw behind the batter on inside pitches, from in front on outside pitches.

If a manager has two or three catchers on the squad, he can drill them as follows:

Have the catchers line up side-by-side with plenty of room between each catcher. Have them face the coach and assume the Receiving Position. The coach can yell out the pitch, then "shift", the signal for the catchers to go through the steps.

"All right boys/' the manager, or coach could say. "It's a right-hand hitter. Get ready for the pitch. Here it comes, *low* and *inside* . . . Ready? SHIFT!"

He can repeat that line with all the variations. The teacher *cannot* spend too much time on this exercise. If a boy is having trouble with the steps, his Dad can help him in the back yard, cellar or attic.

After the Sign Position and Receiving Position have been taught, it's time to think about working behind the plate. Most 8-to-10 year-old catchers take the Receiving Stance much too far back. They are concerned, of course, about having the bat hit their noggins instead of the ball. But, here's something to remember: If the batter can't reach the catcher with his bat on the back swing before the pitch, he won't reach him when he tries to hit the ball. That's because the batter goes forward—away from the catcher—to hit. If a catcher stays just out of reach of the back swing, he's perfectly safe.

But, he must get as close as he possibly can for these reasons: If he's back an extra foot, he makes the pitcher throw an extra foot. If he's back an extra foot, the curve ball will start its break too late. By staying too far back, the catcher adds to the distance of his throw to the bases.

The beginner often closes his eyes when the batter swings at a pitch. He sometimes turns his head, too. Both of these are natural reactions, but dangerous! The catcher won't get hurt, if he keeps his eyes open, chin down and looks straight ahead until the ball is in the glove. His equipment will protect him.

The young catcher, by the way, will also flinch at balls thrown into the dirt. Here again he should use his equipment—drop to the knees, get the glove on the ground and block the ball!

## The Catcher's Throw

Once the basic positions and shifts are taught, it's only natural to start working on the throw itself. Like the outfielders, the catcher must throw overhand with his hand directly behind the ball. He doesn't want the ball to curve and if the ball hits the dirt, he wants good back spin so it will hop high and sharply. Unlike the outfielder, however, the catcher does not have enough time to use a full arm swing. He must use a snap throw. To get the proper position for the throwing arm, hold the arm in the layback position described earlier for the overhand throw. Instead of holding the hand directly over the pitching elbow, bring it down to a spot behind the ear. Now, step forward and "snap"' the ball toward the target. A football player uses the same technique in throwing a spiral forward pass.

The catcher always wants to throw directly at the base to catch a runner stealing. If he's throwing to 2nd on the cut-off play (page 79), he throws directly at the cut-off man's head.

The very first time a catcher puts on a mask, by the way,

he should be taught how to throw the ball to the pitcher correctly!

The pitcher works very hard during a ball game. He shouldn't be put to the added effort of jumping for wild throws from the catcher. (It's not only bad for the pitcher, it's dangerous with runners on base.)

The ball should be thrown at the pitcher's glove shoulder, which, is in a direct line and at just the right height for the throw to 2nd base. The catcher shouldn't lob the ball back to the pitcher, nor should he fire it so hard it gives the pitcher a red hand. A medium speed throw is best-always at the glove shoulder! When the bases are occupied, catchers should form the habit of taking a quick look at the runners before returning the ball to the pitcher.

## The Catcher Fields Too

Like others on the defense, the catcher has an assignment when the ball is hit. Most of the time, it's guarding the plate. On pop-ups and bunts, however, the play for the put-out is very often all his.

No matter what the play, the catcher ought to toss his mask aside as quickly as possible.

To field the bunt, the catcher (presumably right-handed) should always try to go to the left of the ball—make a little circle if he can—so he'll be in good position to throw when he comes up with it. If the ball is still rolling when the catcher reaches it, he should stab his glove down in front of it to stop the roll, then scoop his glove and bare hand together for the pickup. If the ball has stopped, the catcher can make the pickup with the bare hand.

## Catch It With Your Nose

On all pop-ups, the catcher wants to get under the ball as

quickly as he can and be waiting as the ball comes down. Since pop-ups to the catcher are caused by a sharp undercut of the ball, the ball spins at terrific speed. The spin will make the ball "move" in one direction or another but usually toward the infield. The catcher must be careful of this drift as the ball comes down and not try to catch it with the arms extended, else he will suddenly find that his arms are two inches short!

To keep the ball from floating out of reach, the catcher should keep his nose right underneath it. "Catch it with your nose/' the pros say. (It's a good idea, too, to blink eyes rapidly as they follow downward flight of the ball. This helps prevent "blind staggers.")

On pop-ups that go in back of the catcher, the spin caused by the undercut of the bat often makes the ball curve as it goes up. As a general rule, it will curve toward the batter if he undercuts an outside pitch and away from him if the pitch is inside. Thus, if the ball goes up over the catcher's left shoulder, he should turn to his right to go back and under. That way, he will usually find the ball curving toward him, making the catch much easier. If the ball goes up over the right shoulder, the catcher should turn left to chase it.

**Catchers Cover 3rd**

There are three times when the catcher covers 3rd. The first and most important is part of his assignment in the bunt defense with a runner on 1st. (See Fig. 40.) The catcher charges into the diamond on the bunt, but if the third baseman fields the ball, he circles to his left and hustles to 3rd. If he doesn't do that, the base will be open and the runner advancing from 1st to 2nd can continue to 3rd.

The catcher also occasionally finds himself on 3rd during

a run-down between home and 3rd, as described on page 133. He again goes to 3rd when both the shortstop and second baseman chase a pop fly directly in back of 2nd with runners on base. (Third baseman takes 2nd, pitcher covers home.)

It's a good idea for catchers to back up 1st when the bases are unoccupied and the batter hits a grounder to the infield. This is especially important in a close ball game. The catcher, to make this back-up play, should start running at the crack of the bat and head for a spot at least 20 feet to the foul side of 1st. Thus, if the ball gets by the first baseman, the catcher and ball will arrive at about the same time and the catcher will be able to either hold the runner on 1st or nip him going into 2nd if he tries to advance.

## Calling the Pitch

A basic part of the catcher's defensive work is the simple act of giving the signal for the type of pitch he wants thrown to the batter. He doesn't do this casually, though. Like the pitcher, he should always study the hitters to pick out weak and strong points. After playing a team once, the catcher should jot down in a notebook whatever he has learned about the opposing hitters. Before the second game with a team, he and the pitcher ought to go over these notes. That might sound a little too "professional" for youngsters, but it really isn't. As we've pointed out before, the younger the player, the more glaring his weakness. There are some 12-year-olds, for example, who simply cannot hit an outside pitch. And, furthermore, they can't resist swinging at it—even though they can't reach it. We can certainly expect a 12-year-old catcher to remember that kind of a weakness in a hitter.

The catcher can learn a great deal about hitters by watching their foot movements. Does the batter step away from the plate when he strides forward for the swing? If he does, pitch him outside. Does the batter stand too close, or too far away? Is he deep, or up in front of the batter's box? The catcher should look for other clues too. Can the hitter get "around" on the fast ball? Does he wear glasses? Does he have a bad wrist? Is he a nervous hitter? Where does he hit in the batting order? Has he ever gotten a hit off the pitcher? If so, was it a curve ball, or a fast ball?

Oh, yes, there's more to calling for the pitch than just flicking the fingers. But, some of these weaknesses are very
obvious and even the eight to 10-year-old catcher should be taught to observe them and make his pitching signs accordingly.

## Curve Him Joe

At the beginning of this chapter, we talked about the Sign Position and mentioned that the signs for the pitcher— and the rest of the defensive team, by the way—are given with the throwing hand held deep against the crotch. Many young catchers drop the signaling hand so low that the fingers pop out from underneath their tails. When that happens, of course, everyone in the ball park knows whether it's going to be a fast ball or curve. Keep the signaling hand just below the top of the thigh and be sure the glove hides it from the 3rd base coach.

The signals should be simple. It is suggested that the catcher show one finger for the fast ball, two for the curve and waggle the first for a pitch-out. He can sign for high, low, inside or outside pitches by using his thumb. For example, if the catcher shows the index finger, then points his thumb at the batter then at the ground, he's calling for a fast ball, low and inside. Again this may seem too advanced for a 12-year old, but the manager who follows this course, is teaching his catcher and pitcher to *think*. He may not expect the pitcher to put the ball low and inside, but he's making him *try.*

With a runner on 2nd base, the catcher must change his tactics. The runner can see the sign as easily as the pitcher and he can relay it to the batter.

From high school on up to professional ball, catchers give signs in a "series" with a runner on 2nd. Prior to the game catcher and pitcher may decide:

In a series of three, the sign that shows up once, is the sign that counts. (If the catcher signs 1, then 2 fingers and again 2 fingers, he's calling for a fast ball. If he signs 1-1-2, he's calling for a curve ball.)

In a series of three, the sign that shows up twice, is the sign that counts. (If the catcher flashes 2-2-1, he's calling for a curve ball, etc.).

In a series of three, the middle sign counts (or the first or the third).

## Light and Dark

To keep runners from stealing signs, the receiver uses two other methods. One is called "light and dark." If the catcher holds the glove elbow away from the body, the pitcher can see daylight between the arm and body. That could mean the curve or fast ball, whichever the battery mates agree upon. If the elbow is against the body—"dark"— it could also mean "curve" or "fast ball." The catcher some-times uses his glove for the sign. If the glove is held with the little finger pointing down, as it normally is, that's the fast ball. If turned so that the palm faces the ground, that could be the signal for the curve.

Naturally, if the catcher uses "light and dark" or the glove, he still gives signs, false ones, with his throwing hand.

## Covering the Plate

Catchers and managers should pay particular attention to the fundamentals involved in guarding home plate against the runner trying to score. The catcher wants to "know" where the plate is located as he watches the ball wing toward him from the outfield or infield. To do this, he should straddle the plate. If the ball is hit to right, the catcher leaves the right field corner open. This forces the runner to slide in front of the catcher, with only a small area of the plate to touch. If the ball is hit to left, the catcher again faces the throw, but leaves the left field corner of the plate open. (Figs. 24, 25) The catcher—like the second baseman—should never stand in front of the plate to await the throw, nor should he stand up the line toward third.

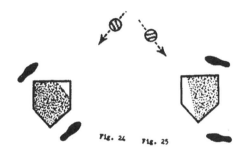

Fig. 24     Fig. 25

At left, catcher leaves corner of plate open as he awaits throw from RF. Third base side of plate is left open when throw is from LF.

This writer never likes to use the term "block the plate" when teaching catchers. It gives catchers the impression they are to hold the runner off. If a catcher attempts to stand between home plate and the runner with, or without the ball, he's going to get hurt. The runner has no place to go, but right through the catcher. Very often, the runner won't slide because there's no room to slide. Furthermore, if the catcher doesn't have the ball in his possession and the runner makes contact with him, the runner scores on the interference rule.

## Play the Ball - Then the Man

Give the runner a place to slide. If the throw is late or wild, go after the ball and forget the runner. If you have the ball in time and the runner slides, block the foot reaching for the base with a knee. If the ball is coming from right field, drop the left knee—after the runner starts his slide, not before. If the throw is coming from left field, drop the right knee.

Naturally, the throw isn't always going to be exactly where the catcher wants it. Ball and runner occasionally arrive at the same spot at the same instant. This may mean a collision. Again, though, the catcher should not try to hold the runner back. If the runner is standing up, he should make the tag and roll *with* the runner—letting the runner turn him around. If the runner is sliding, the catcher should drop on top of him.

On all tags, the catcher should turn the back of the glove toward the runner. (Reasons are explained in 2nd base play.)

When the bases are loaded, the catcher doesn't need to make a tag. With less than two out, the play is often home-to-first.

After catching an infielder's throw, the catcher must make the put-out and relay to 1st without hitting the batter.

To accomplish this easily, the catcher puts his left foot on one side of home base and faces the fielder. After the catch, he steps forward with his right foot, pivots right and throws to the first baseman, who should be standing well inside the line with his left foot on the inside edge of 1st base.

## Know the Pitchers

The catcher, in addition to learning the mechanics of his

job, also has to know something about "handling" pitchers. He must get to know their capabilities, what kind of temperament they have, etc. If the pitcher is a very nervous boy and inclined to pitch too fast, it's up to the catcher to hold the ball longer between pitches and slow him down. If the pitcher gets discouraged quickly, the catcher ought to talk to him and try to keep his spirits up.

Most of all, the catcher ought to know which pitch is the hurler's best—is it the fast ball, or the curve? {The "best" on the day he's pitching).

When a new pitcher comes into the game, the catcher meets him at the mound, reviews the signs, the current situation, the number of outs, the score and the next hitter.

### Be The Quarterback

The catcher, like the hitter, is within the vision of every defensive player. This puts him in position to "take charge" of the ball club in the field. And "take charge" he must. Part of his assignment is to see to it that every boy is playing in the right position for the hitter. He moves the outfield to left or right; brings the infield up or directs it to play back. If he's not fielding a bunt, he tells the boy who does where to throw the ball. He decides whether a ground ball is to be played home-to-1st (with bases loaded), or whether the infield is to try for a 2nd-to-1st double play. The infield in particular has to know in advance where to make the play with runners on base. It's up to the catcher to tell them— whether he decides on his own, or gets his orders from the manager.

### Wear Equipment Correctly

It's not a good idea for the catcher to let anyone else use his mitt. That's his most important tool and it needs to be in perfect condition at all times. Break it in yourself, catcher, and it will fit your hand. Don't use a sponge unless you have a sore hand. In other words, try to toughen up the catching hand so you won't need a sponge.

Buckle the shinguards with buckles on the outside. That way they won't catch when you're running. When your team is at bat, don't take the shinguards off unless you are among the first three hitters.

Don't wear the chest protector loose, it will hamper throws to the bases. Keep it under the chin while catching to protect the Adam's Apple. Always wear it the same way; that is, with the buckle on the same side.

Be sure the mask fits snugly. Keep the straps over the ears the protect against foul tips. Keep the leather of the mask clean.

Never go behind the bat without *full* equipment!

**Chapter 6**

# First Base Play

On a ball hit to any infielder, the first baseman hustles quickly to the bag to establish himself as a target. He wants to catch the ball as soon as possible and, simultaneously, tag the base for the put-out. He will be knocked down by the runner, however, if he stands on top of the base. If he stands in back of the base and the runner passes between him and the thrown ball, the ball is apt to hit the runner and the put-out opportunity will be lost. The only logical place to stand and receive the ball is in front of the base.

As soon as the first baseman determines that he will not be fielding the ball, he runs to the base, placing his feet so the heels touch the side nearest the fielder. In this position, he doesn't have to turn his head away from the fielder to locate the base. He *knows* where it is. He also knows the

First baseman races to cover bag when ball is hit to any other infield position. Note placement of feet.

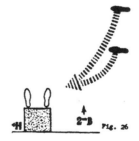

**runner has room to cross the bag. Thus, he need only concentrate on the throw.**

When catching the ball, the first baseman should never let one foot cross the position of the other. He should make what is known as a "three-step" move. If the ball is to the right, the first baseman takes a short step to the right with his right foot. He then places his left foot against the perpendicular inside surface of the bag—still leaving the entire top of the base free for the runner. To complete the move, he takes a big step forward with the right foot while pushing away from the bag with the left. The maneuver is repeated to the left, when the ball is thrown to the left. When catching a ball directly in front, the right-handed first baseman should start his three-step move with his left foot. Thus, his feet are in proper position to make a throw. The reverse applies if the first baseman is left-handed.

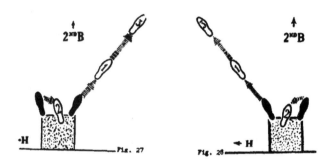

**In sketch above left, first baseman makes three-step move to right. Move to left is shown in next sketch.**

On high throws that can be caught in front of the base, the first sacker has no choice but to reach as high as he can to make the catch. High throws out of reach in front of the base can sometimes be caught in back of the bag or in foul ground. In this case, the first baseman should skip across the base into foul ground, with his toes touching the bag. If he can catch the ball with a stretch, fine. If not, he should jump, make the catch and kick the outside of the base as he comes down (still leaving the top of the bag free).

On wild throws, the first baseman—and this applies to any baseman—should forget the base and concentrate on catching, or knocking the ball down.

Occasionally, an infielder will throw the ball on the home plate side of 1st and too wide for a normal put-out. The first baseman should forget the bag, make the catch and try to tag the runner.

The first baseman should play any ground ball he thinks lie can reach (again, this applies to any fielder). If he fields a ball deep to his right with 1st unoccupied, he should toss the ball to the pitcher, whose job is to cover the bag. If he can make the put-out himself by running to the base and touching it, he should do so and wave the pitcher off. Never risk a throw if it's not necessary.

Assuming, however, that the first baseman has fielded a ball far to his right, he still has a tricky job ahead of him—getting the ball to the pitcher who is dashing over to cover 1st. The first baseman wants to pass the ball to the pitcher *quickly* and yet make the throw easy to handle. A fairly hard, underhand toss that is chest high and "leads" the pitcher will do the job nicely. The throwing hand, however, ought to be away from the body. If the throwing hand is in line with the body, the white ball will blend with the light-colored uniform and the pitcher may lose sight of it. (If the first baseman is more than 25 feet away from the pitcher, he should throw overhand.)

On balls hit to his left, he can continue left and touch the base.

On throws from the catcher on bunts or topped balls in fair territory, the first baseman should put his left foot against the 2nd base side of 1st base and make the target well to the inside. On throws from behind the plate, the first baseman makes his target in foul territory, with his right foot on the foul side of 1st base.

### With A Runner On First

These maneuvers change with a runner on 1st. If the ball is hit to the right, the first baseman should field the ball and fire to 2nd for the double play (less than two out). The left-handed first baseman has an advantage here—he doesn't have to pivot to make the throw to 2nd. The right-hander, however, after fielding the ball, must pivot right (left side facing 2nd base) to throw. After throwing, he should hustle to 1st to catch the return throw and complete the DP. If the second baseman is there to handle the throw, however, he should duck out of the way.

On balls hit far to his left with a runner on 1st, the first baseman should start the double play in "reverse." Rather than stop, pivot and try to throw to 2nd, he can continue to 1st, touch the base to retire the batsman, then throw on to 2nd. The second baseman, with the "force" removed, however, must now tag the runner coming down from 1st.

### Holding The Runner

Keeping the runner close to the base is one of the first sacker's biggest assignments in leagues in which stealing is permitted. While it appears to be a routine chore, it must never be treated routinely. The first baseman must constantly "play the runner" on all but two occasions—when 2nd base is occupied and when his team is so far in front that one run for the team at bat is unimportant.

For all right-hand hitters, the first baseman can play the runner by taking a position at the bag and inside the imaginary line that runs between 1st and 2nd. With a left-hand hitter at the plate, he plays in his normal fielding position, but before and after the pitch darts to the bag to worry the runner, or take a throw.

With a right-hander at bat, the right-handed first baseman straddles the corner of the base that points to 3rd. His right foot and leg does not block the base, but leaves at least half of it open so the runner leading away has a clear

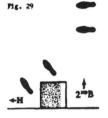

Fig. 29

**Right hand first baseman stands as indicated to hold runner close to base.**

return path. This first baseman faces the general direction of the shortstop which permits him to see the pitcher clearly, yet reach the open part of the base with his glove hand. The left-handed first baseman can put his right foot on the home plate side of the base and have his body turned more to the right.

Whether right-handed, or left-handed, the first baseman wants to catch the ball and make the tag in one motion. A down-and-back sweep of the arm brings the glove to the ground on the open side of the base, forcing the runner to tag himself out as he returns.

When the first baseman realizes his pitcher is going to throw the ball to the batter, he hustles to his fielding position. When the ball goes *by* the batter, he returns quickly to the defensive post at the bag.

Note: Other 1st base assignments will be discussed in later chapters.

# Chapter 7

# Second Base Play

The second baseman has to be the most agile, acrobatic individual on the ball club. No other player, in carrying out his assignment, need shift direction as sharply, quickly and as many times as the second sacker. It's "Jack be nimble, Jack be quick" every moment.

Our second sacker is the key to the double play, one of the most powerful defensive maneuvers in baseball. That's why old-time sportswriters often referred to him as "guardian of the keystone."

We're going to concentrate here on the footwork used to make the DP from this strategically important infield position. Primarily, three things are involved: Get to the base quickly so the shortstop or third baseman doesn't have to hold up his throw. Tag the base while in possession of the ball. Make a strong throw from a point *away* from the base.

The third item, of course, is the toughest, although the professionals make it look easy. The professional can use six or more different steps to make the DP. The amateur should learn at least three.

The spot where the shortstop fields the ball generally tells the second baseman which step he must use; it indicates whether he is to go "inside" the diamond to make his throw, "out" (toward center field), or "back" (toward right field).

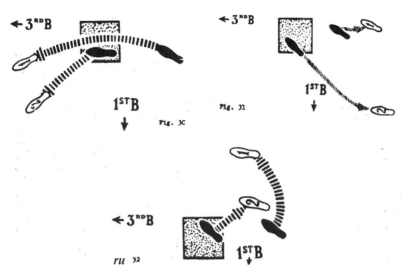

Second baseman uses several combinations of steps to make a put-out and relay of ball to 1st for DP. Above left to right are steps used to go "inside", "back". Sketch below shows how player goes "out" to avoid runner.

To go "inside," the second baseman puts his left foot on the bag and propels his body into the diamond as far as possible. Naturally, he lands on his right foot. As he does so, he shifts his weight to that right foot, then strides left toward 1st and makes the throw.

To go "back," the second baseman puts his left foot against the bag. After catching the ball for the put-out, he pushes back into right field, landing on the right foot, stepping left for the throw.

He can go "out" by placing the left foot against the center field side of the base; pushing toward center after the catch, landing right and stepping left to throw.

Some managers first teach the second baseman to step on 2nd base with the right foot and to throw off that foot.

This may be alright if the ball arrives at 2nd long before the runner. If it's going to be close, however, the second baseman will often find the runner between him and 1st, blocking both his vision and throw. In addition, he's apt to be knocked down by the runner.

All of these moves should be part of a continuous motion. If, however, the second baseman gets to the base and the shortstop fumbles the ball, he can straddle the base with the left foot on the 1st base side and the right foot on the opposite side. (Like the first baseman, he has to "know" where the base is while awaiting the throw.) When he catches the ball in this position, he can touch the bag with the inside of his left foot and throw off the right. If the runner is sliding (as he should be on a close play), he can raise the left leg to "let the runner in." With the base between the runner and the throwing foot, the second baseman avoids being spiked, or otherwise injured. (When there's no opportunity or need to throw to 1st, second sacker can play the base as the first baseman would, pushing toward the throw.)

But, you ask, when does he make which move?

As noted the fielding point is usually the tip-off. If the ball is fielded well inside the imaginary line between 2nd and 3rd, the second baseman can best make the play by going "inside." If the ball is fielded deep, he should go "back" or "out." If the ball is fielded close to the line, it's optional. The throw, too, sometimes directs the move. If it's wide to the centerfield side, the second baseman may be forced to go "out." If wide to the inside, he cannot very well go "out" or "back."

Actually, we've discussed last things first in describing these steps. One must not overlook the importance of getting *to* the base to receive the throw. If anything, the young second baseman should do his best to be at the base *waiting* for the toss. He must also be sure to avoid making his put-out "on the grass," as the umpires say. He's got to have part of his body touching the base when he catches the ball.

## "Throw Wild To The Glove Side"

The first throw is as important as any other phase of the double play. It should be aimed at the glove shoulder. As the pros say—"If you must throw wild—throw wild to the glove side!" That means that if the infielder has to hurry, he should "hurry" to the glove side, where his teammate has a chance to get the ball. If the ball goes to the barehand side, the receiver rarely can make the catch. Every fielder must keep in mind that it is of utmost importance to put out the *lead* runner. Be *sure* of that one! Look on the relay to 1st for the second out as a bonus. When close to the bag, the second baseman should use an underhand toss with a little "mustard" on it (force). Again, like the first baseman, he should "show the ball" by keeping the throwing hand away from the body.

If 2nd base is only a step or two away, the second base-man should wave the shortstop off, tag the base, then throw to 1st.

## Other Duties

The second baseman has specific assignments on infield flies, bunts, steals and extra base hits. While all of these responsibilities are touched on in other sections of the book, it might be well to go over them here.

The second baseman is to field all fly balls from short center to the short right field fence and everything to the mound in front of his normal field position. On any fly ball deep to the area described, he starts *immediately,* deter-mined to catch the ball. That's his territory. He never gives lip on the ball unless an outfielder calls for the catch] The outfielder always has the "right of way" as he is in a much better position to catch the ball, view the situation in the infield and make a throw.

It is also most important for the first baseman and second baseman to understand that balls directly behind the first baseman are the second baseman's responsibility (unless, of course, the first baseman need only take a few steps back to make the catch).

After catching a "pop fly" with men on base, the infielder must quickly get into position to throw in case a runner breaks. He must be careful, however, not to be bluffed into throwing the ball unnecessarily. The best practice is to catch the ball, hold on to it and run rapidly to the mound. (See Chapter 18.)

## Steals

Protecting the bag against the first-to-second base steal is another big job for the second baseman. With a runner on 1st, it's best if he shortens up his position, so he can get to the base ahead of the catcher's throw. If the batter hits consistently to right (regardless of whether he is right or left-handed) he should have the shortstop take the throw, wait for the ball to pass the batter, then race to his right to back up the shortstop.

When covering the base on steals, the second baseman straddles the base, facing the catcher. His toes are even with the corner that points into center field.

Many beginners form the bad habit of standing to the home plate side of 2nd to receive the catcher's throw. Even if the throw is good, he will not have much of a chance of getting the tag on the runner from this position.

Young second basemen are also inclined to move into the diamond toward the throw if it seems to be low enough to

Baseman should always leave corner of base open when awaiting ball to make tag on approaching runner. At right, second baseman defends against steal and awaits throw from RF.

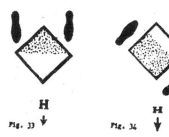

H

Fig. 33 ↓

H

Fig. 34 ↓

hit the dirt. This again is a mistake. He should hold his position behind the base. If the ball bounces with any force, he will have a chance to tag the runner. Like any other fielder, however, the second baseman should forget the base and go after the ball if (a) it's obvious that the runner has the throw beaten, or (b) the throw is wild.

The technique for making the tag is the same for the second baseman as for any other infielder and the same general principles apply. The infielder must never try to hold the runner back with the ball. He ought to make the tag firmly, to be sure, but the tagging hand should ride *with* the runner's body. Secondly, the infielder should place his feet in such a way as to leave one side or one corner of the base open. By doing so, he encourages the runner to slide to the open spot. That way, the infielder can have his head turned away from the runner as he watches the ball and still know, in advance, where to make the tag. His objective *is* to catch the ball and, with a quick sweep of the arm and hand, lay the ball on the open side of the base, forcing the runner to tag himself out.

The infielder must never try to make a high tag on a sliding runner. The thing to keep in mind is this: To be safe, the runner must touch the base. The base is on the ground-not in the air above it. An infielder, to make this point even clearer, may make a nice tag on a runner's chest, but it does him no good if the runner's feet (the part of the body to arrive first) have already gone by and made contact with the base.

When making the tag, by the way, the infielder will be able to control the ball better if the back of the glove hand faces the oncoming runner. With the palm of the glove hand facing the runner, the runner's feet are apt to strike above the wrist, snap the hand up and cause the ball to pop out.

## Holding The Runner

When playing a runner leading away from the base, any infielder has these objectives—catch the runner off the base; make the runner run the full 90 feet to the next base. The latter objective is very important at 2nd, because it is the spot from which a runner can score on a good single.

The runner leading away from 2nd usually has the second baseman in his field of vision. If the second baseman bluffs a run for the bag, the runner will see him and start for the base. By the same token, if the second baseman doesn't pay any attention to the runner, he gives the runner an opportunity to stretch his lead.

While the second baseman does not always have a good chance to work a pickoff play with the pitcher, he can decoy the runner into such a play for the shortstop. Visualize this:

Runner and second baseman on the bag just before the pitcher steps on the rubber. Pitcher stretches. Second baseman moves to his position. Runner leads away. Pitcher waits. Second baseman runs back to bag, runner returns to bag.

As the second baseman turns his back on the runner and returns to his position, the runner instinctively leads off. At this instant, the shortstop rushes to the base, the pitcher whirls and throws. The shortstop is back of the runner and out of his field of vision, thus the runner must rely on the voice signal of the third base coach to realize he's in danger. If the play works, the defense has an out. If not, it has put enough pressure on the runner to keep him reasonably close to the bag.

The second baseman returns to the base after every pitch and does not leave again until the pitcher is on the rubber. Then he should always move to keep pressure on the runner.

Cut It!

With runners on 1st and 3rd in anything below the high school level of ball the defense has a tough problem. If the runner on 1st breaks for 2nd and the catcher makes his throw to 2nd, the runner on 3rd can usually score. In college or professional ball, the second baseman can often go to the base to play the runner going from 1st to 2nd. Then, if he sees the runner on 3rd try for home, he probably has enough power in his throwing arm to fire to the plate to catch him.

But, in the younger groups, second basemen rarely have that power. Here's a cut-off play that will help the defense in this situation.

The offense, first of all, will probably order the runner to steal on the 1st pitch and have the batter "take" to avoid a double play on a line drive. If the defense expects the play, the pitcher should "pitch out", giving the catcher a good chance to get the ball away to 2nd.

The second baseman, instead of going to the 2nd, runs to a spot halfway between the mound and the bag and on a direct line between 2nd and home. The shortstop covers 2nd, the third baseman 3rd. The catcher fires right at the second baseman's head.

If the runner on 3rd does not break, the shortstop yells "Let It Go!" The second baseman does and ducks out of the way.

If the runner on 3rd is breaking, the shortstop should yell "Cut It!" The second baseman cuts the ball off and throws to the plate. There are these "ifs":

If the runner going from 3rd to home stops halfway down the line—charge him.

If the catcher's throw is off line, cut it off whether the runner on 3rd goes or not.

Relays

Every time a batter gets a base hit, the second baseman has a specific assignment—a spot to run to. The situation tells him in advance where that spot will be.

For example:

Any time there is a runner on 1st, 1st and 2nd, or 1st, 2nd, or 3rd and the batter get's a single, there's only one place for the second baseman to go—2nd base.

If there's no one on and the ball is singled to right, the shortstop takes the base, with the second baseman in a position some 15 feet away in a direct line with the fielder. The second baseman does this to shorten up the outfielder's throw and make sure that it is handled "clean." After catching the ball, he runs it into the diamond.

If there's no one on and the ball is singled to left, the reverse applies; second baseman takes the bag and shortstop goes out to get the ball.

Now then, if the ball goes for more than a single in the right half of the diamond, the second baseman must hustle to the outfield to help bring the ball in and try to catch the runner. This is called the "relay" play. It works this way:

As soon as the second baseman realizes that the ball is riding for extra bases, he should turn and run—and really run!—toward the outfielder. If the ball appears to be settling 100 feet beyond the second baseman's position, he should come to a stop about 50 feet out. Judging depth will be no problem for the second baseman if he starts running *immediately, runs hard* and says to himself:

"I will stop just before the outfielder picks up the ball."

On receiving the ball from the outfielder, the second baseman should also say to himself, "I am now an outfielder and I must throw like an outfielder; directly overhand and with full power."

When the ball is cracked for extra bases to the left half of the diamond, the second baseman covers 2nd base and the shortstop becomes the relay man.

There are two things about the preceding explanation that may arouse some argument. One involves the batted ball that goes for a double. In professional ranks, the second baseman, because of his vast experience and the throwing power of the outfielders, will go directly to the bag on hits to the right side with the shortstop backing up.

With players of up to high school age, it is a much better practice to have the second baseman go to the relay post on *all* extra base hits to right. This makes up for lack of throwing power on the part of the outfielder and also eliminates the possibility of indecision or confusion on the part of an inexperienced second baseman. (The outfielder, by the way, can still throw directly to 2nd if he so chooses.)

The other point involves the relay itself. Many managers emphasize that the first throw should be the longer of the two relay tosses. This writer has found that the young out-fielder has trouble judging distance in this situation and, if anything, the first throw should be somewhat shorter than the second. If the infielder is to have any chance at all, the first throw has to be a hard strike to the infielder's chest If the first throw is weak, low, or off line, the opportunity for a put-out is lost at the very start of the play.

## Backing Up Bases

If infield practice is conducted properly (see Chapter 25), the second, baseman will have no difficulty learning to back up the proper base. Here are the usual back-up situations:

Catcher to first baseman covering 1st (on "topped" balls, bunts, wild pitches, passed balls)

Shortstop to first baseman on double play.

Pitcher to first baseman on balls hit to left of pitcher

Catcher to pitcher when bases loaded and score is close

Cutoff man (first baseman) to shortstop covering $2^{nd}$

In backing up any play, the second baseman—or any fielder—should run to a point at least 20 feet in back of the base. Thus, if the ball goes by the person covering the bag, the boy backing up will have enough room to see and field it. If the second baseman moves to back up a base and finds it uncovered, he should quickly go in and play the base.

The second baseman covers 1st base on all bunts (See Figs. 40, 41.) He must not leave his position, however until he's sure the batter intends to lay the ball down. After retiring a bunter at 1st, he should quickly run the ball to the mound.

**Chapter 8**

# The Shortstop

The shortstop, a combination of infielder and outfielder, is normally the best all-around infielder on the club. To do his job well, he needs good hands, a powerful arm and sprinter's legs. Like the second baseman, he has to be agile and quick. And he has to know how to make the double play!

The shortstop doesn't have as much trouble making the DP as the second baseman because he's traveling in the general direction he has to throw and he has the fielder, the runner and 1st base in front of him. Still, he ought to have a combination of steps that permit him to tag the base and effectively fire the ball to 1st.

The simplest way for the shortstop to start the DP is for him to put his right foot on the sack, hop to the right field side of the base, pivoting the body right at the same time. He should land on his right foot for the throw. Follow these instructions and you'll get the idea:

Stand on the right [foot only. Hop on it. Hop forward on it. Now, hop forward on it and turn the body a quarter to the right.

This time, step forward left, step forward right, hop, make the pivot right, land light and throw.

A shortstop crossing the base at fair running speed can put himself completely out of the baseline with this move and make a strong, fast throw.

A variation, called the "drag" step (used by most professionals) will also take the shortstop out of the baseline nicely. A boy can surely learn it by the time he's 13 or 14. Here's the way it works:

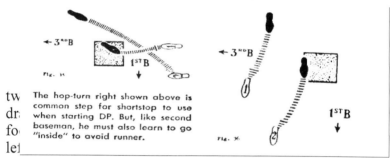

tw
dr
fo
lef

The hop-turn right shown above is common step for shortstop to use when starting DP. But, like second baseman, he must also learn to go "inside" to avoid runner.

To make this move while running is tricky, so try it while walking at first. Time the steps so that the left foot comes down in back of the base, but slightly to the right field side. As the right foot is brought in contact with the base and passes behind the left, pivot the body sharply to the right. To make the pivot, the shortstop hops off his left foot and brings his right foot up to replace it.

So, it's step over or in back of the base with the left; drag the right foot against the bag; pivot-hop with the left, land right and throw.

The shortstop usually uses the two moves described when the ball is fielded deep by the second or first basemen. If the ball is fielded on the infield grass, he may want to make his throw from the 3rd base side of 2nd. To do this, he should place his left foot against the 3rd base side of the bag, push the body right, land right and throw.

As indicated earlier, the throw to the man covering 2nd to start the DP is extremely important. The shortstop's throw is to the glove shoulder of the second baseman. If this seems too tough a requirement for the very young player—say the nine-year old—the manager still should insist that the ball be thrown at the chest. The shortstop should be more concerned with being *sure* of the first out in the DP situation than the second.

Like the second baseman, the shortstop has a specific assignment on every kind of a base hit. With no one on and a single to the right, he covers 2nd. With no one on and a single to left, he goes out 10 or 15 feet to get the throw from the outfielder. On extra base hits to right, he covers 2nd and directs the second baseman's throw. On extra base hits to left, he hustles out for the relay. He works with the second baseman in holding a runner on 2nd. He protects &nd against steals if he and the second baseman agree that the batter is likely to hit the ball to right. He does all of these things With the same methods described for 2nd base play.

There are some items, however, that are unique. With a runner on 1st in a bunt situation, the shortstop covers 2nd. (He does not leave his position, however, until he's *positive* a bunt attempt will be made.) With runners on 1st and 2nd and a bunt developing, the shortstop has another duty: he must hold the lead runner as close to 2nd as possible and still protect his normal position in the event the batter is not bunting but hitting away. Since the second baseman has to cover 1st on the bunt, the shortstop cannot get any help from him in holding the runner, which is very important in this particular situation. It's the objective of the defense, you see, to try to get a force-out at third, then go to 1st to get the man who bunted the ball. Since this bunt situation usually comes up with none out, the defense, if successful, will have a runner on 2nd with two out after the play. If they cannot get the runner going to 3rd, they generally wind up with a runner on 2nd and 3rd and one out. This means that a good single will score two runs. To get back to the shortstop:

He wants the lead runner to travel the *full distance* to 3rd. Up to high school age level, it's a good idea to have the shortstop play on the base or directly in back of the base in this situation before the ball is pitched. As soon as the shortstop is certain the ball will be pitched, he races to his normal position to protect against a hit. After the ball is in the catcher's hands, he again goes back to 2nd to hold the runner.

The shortstop has still another assignment—that of a cut-off man. With a runner on 1st he moves quickly to the cut-off spot whenever the batter hits a single to any part of the diamond. (See Chapter 15.) If the ball is hit to right and gets by the outfielder, he should leave the cut-off spot immediately and go to 2nd base. If the single gets by an outfielder in left, he leaves the cut-off spot and races out for a possible relay.

When there's a runner on 1st and 2nd and the batter hits a single, the shortstop, obviously, will not be sure whether the outfielder will throw to 3rd or home. If the throw goes to the plate, he should leave the cut-off spot, and run to the back-up position behind 2nd base. All of these moves will become routine for the shortstop if the manager drills the outfield and infield properly.

If you recall, we said the second baseman covers 1st on all bunts. The shortstop covers 2nd on all bunts but one-the squeeze bunt. On the squeeze, he has to cover 3rd in the event the ball is popped into the air by the batter—which gives the defense a chance for a double play—or in case the runner gets close to the plate, stops and decides to return to 3rd.

The shortstop, too, has definite back-up assignments. Here's a list of most of them.

Back up almost all throws to the second baseman as he covers 2nd.

Back up almost all throws to the third baseman as he covers 3rd.

Back up almost all hits to the third baseman.

We use the word "almost" because the shortstop may somehow be involved in another part of the play. The "must" back up plays, however, become obvious during the infield and outfield drills.

The shortstop is also responsible for any fly ball that is falling in the area of his general position, in back of the third baseman, in short left and left center.

# Chapter 9

# Third Base Play

The boy who plays 3rd base need not be as fast a runner as the second baseman or shortstop, but he cannot have lead in his feet or slow hands and do a good job at that spot. Furthermore, he needs a strong and accurate arm and he wants to be as good on ground balls and pop-ups as anyone else in the infield.

With no one on, the third baseman's normal fielding position is about six feet back of 3rd and about 10 feet inside the line. With a runner on 1st, he probably should move in a few steps to have a better chance at the double play. If he suspects a bunt, his standing position should be parallel to the base.

With a runner on 3rd, the third baseman should be almost parallel to the base and eight to ten feet inside the line. This is the best spot from which to handle throws—not in front and not behind. Runner or no runner, however, the third baseman's big job is to "guard the line". Any ball that gets by him along the foul line is usually good for two bases.

Third base is often called the "hot corner" because a great many batted balls travel toward 3rd at terrific speed. Because of this, infield play at 3rd is somewhat different from other positions. On hard smashes the third baseman can use a "trap" position. He sits on his heels, puts his glove on the ground with elbows between the knees and leans forward slightly. If directly in front of the ball in this position, the

Third baseman often uses "trap" position to field hot smashes.

Fig. 37

third baseman can block it, or field it cleanly then hop up and throw.

Handling the bunt is another tough play for the third baseman. He must, first of all, always be alert to the possibility of a bunt. If he suspects one is coming, he should "cheat" a little—move closer to the plate. As the bunt becomes obvious, he is to move quickly to the area he is responsible for in the bunt defense. On the squeeze bunt, a bunt for a base hit with none on, or a sacrifice attempt with a runner on 1st base, the third baseman ought to charge the plate with all speed. With a runner on 1st and 2nd, or just on 2nd, the third baseman cannot drive all the way in until the ball goes by the pitcher.

In this spot, by the way, the third baseman wants to form the habit of hustling to the base *every time* the ball gets by the batter to protect against a fake bunt and steal.

Getting *to* the ball on a bunt is one thing. Picking up the ball and throwing the runner out is quite another. Very often, in fielding the bunt, the third baseman has to throw tile ball while on the run. This requires a good deal of skill and constant practice.

If the ball is moving very fast, the third baseman must use his glove to field it, making the pick-up in front of the body, but slightly to the right side. If he has time, he should stop, straighten up and throw. Mostly, however, he will have to continue running and throw while doubled over.

He must *never, never* attempt this throw unless he's sure he has a chance to get the runner. A wild throw down the right field line may mean one, two or even three runs or two bases for the batter.

On bunted balls that are moving slowly or have stopped, the third baseman should run to the left of the ball and make the pick-up with his bare hand. He should time his steps so that the left foot comes down next to the ball when it's picked up. To practice this play, place about a dozen baseballs from right to left in a straight line and about six inches apart. Put a fielder 25 feet away from each end of the line of balls. With the other infielders, form a line, one behind the other, at right angles to the line of balls and some 25 to 30 feet away. If each player runs to the left end of the line of balls, he can pretend he's the third baseman picking up a bunt to throw to 1st. The line should then form on the opposite side of the string of replaced balls. Repeat the drill by throwing to the second fielder. (It is advisable for all infielders to participate in the drill, by the way.)

The third sacker plays everything he can reach to his left, just as the first baseman drives for every ball he thinks he can reach to his right. This means, of course, that he will often cut the ball off in front of the shortstop. With runners on 1st and 2nd and less than two out and the ball driven sharply to his right, the third baseman continues to the bag after catching the ball, steps on it then throws to 1st. He does the same thing with two outs (steps on 3rd) in this situation, or with one out and the bases loaded (steps on 3rd, throws to 1st). With the bases loaded and the ball hit so that the third baseman can field it while going toward the plate, the play should be third-to-home-to-first (assuming score is close. If defensive team is ahead or far behind, play can go third-to-second-to-first). With two outs and bases loaded, play should almost always go to first as the batter has the longest distance to run and the third out nullifies any run crossing the plate.

Like the other infielders, the third baseman has a specific area to cover on fly balls to the left side of the diamond. Balls that drop in fair or foul ground halfway between 3rd and home are the responsibility of the third baseman. He is also responsible for any ball that falls in the general area of his position and any ball he can reach that drops beyond 3rd to his right. Fly balls that come down directly behind him should be left for the shortstop to handle.

In professional ball, the third baseman is often used as a cut-off man on hits to left. It is better, however, for the first baseman to act as cut-off man on all throws from the outfield on teams of up to high school age. This means the third baseman has only one place to go on base hits—3rd base!

## "Look" The Runner Back

The younger third baseman often forgets to "hold" runners at 2nd or 3rd after fielding the ball. For example, if there's a runner on 2nd, less than two out, and an easy bouncer is hit to the third baseman, he should, after picking up the ball, "look" at the runner leading away from 2nd. That look is usually enough to make the runner stay where he is.

A somewhat similar situation develops at 3rd with a runner who has a big lead. After fielding the ball, the third baseman may not only find it necessary to look, but to hold the ball for a few seconds. It's not a difficult play—just a matter of forming the proper habit.

There are probably more line drives hit to the 3rd base area than to any other section of the diamond. Usually, as the ball is hit, the runners will instinctively break. Just as on a fly ball, the fielder can put the runner out if he can get the ball to the base before the runner can return to it. Thus, with less than two out and one base occupied, the third baseman, after catching the line drive, should immediately whip the ball to that base. With 1st and 3rd occupied, he should throw to 1st if the ball is hit to his left, try to step on 3rd if hit to his right. With 1st and 2nd occupied, or the bases loaded, he should go to 2nd on balls hit to his left, try to step on 3rd and throw to 2nd on balls hit fat enough to his right. In the latter situation, if there are none out, there's the possibility of a triple play

On tag plays at 3rd, the boy who covers that sack should straddle the base, facing 2nd. His feet should be in foul ground. He now knows where the runner will slide and should lay the back side of the glove against the base in the path of the runner's tagging foot.

There are three occasions for the third baseman to back up team-mates normally—on a rundown between 3rd and home and possibly between 3rd and 2nd, and whenever the first baseman throws the ball to the pitcher in a bases loaded situation. There's occasion, too, for the third baseman to cover another base. He goes to 2nd if the second baseman and shortstop are after a pop fly in back of 2nd. (In that case, catcher covers 3rd).

# Chapter 10

# Outfield Play

A ball club's outfield has three major assignments when in the field:

1. Take a base hit away from a batter whenever possible. (Catch the fly ball).

2. Cut down the length of base hits. (Hustle and work together to hold the batter and/or runners to the minimum number of bases).

3. Keep runners from advancing whenever possible. (Throw to the right base; throw strongly and accurately).

Every move the outfielder makes has one of the three points we've named as its objective. These suggestions will help:

The outfielder, to repeat a point, should watch the batter and not the pitcher, as the ball is being delivered to the plate. His line of vision should be so adjusted that the top of the batter's head comes just under the peak of the put-fielder's cap. (New hats have a little fuzz along the under edge. This should be burned off).

As the batter strides to hit, the outfielder leans forward slightly, raises the heels off the ground and takes one small step forward. He should listen to the sound of the bat meeting ball. With a little experience it will tell him how well the ball has been hit.

On balls driven to right or left, the outfielder uses the "cross-over" step. If he's going to his right, his first move is to pivot right and take the first step toward the ball with his left foot. The opposite to the opposite side.

The outfielder *always* breaks fast! On fly balls to his area, he should not—as he starts—try to time his approach to the arrival of the ball. After the '"jump", with runners on base, the outfielder can use some momentum to make a throw. But, if no throw is going to be involved, he wants to be waiting to catch the ball when it comes down. A slow-starting, lazy outfielder is a threat to the success of the ball club.

To catch the ball, outfielders—any fielder, for that matter —ought to use both hands if possible. With runners on base, balls above the waist should be caught with the thumbs together and fingers pointing up; below the waist with little fingers together and fingers pointing down. If there is no one on base and the outfielder is camped under a high fly ball, he should catch the ball with the backs of his hands facing the ground and held close to the body.

When a fly ball is hit over an outfielder's head, he should turn his back to the plate. If it's not going to be too deep, he can watch it over his shoulder as he runs. If he judges that the ball is really going for a ride, he should take his eyes off it and concentrate on running, then look back for the ball.

As the outfielder runs, by the way, he should stay on his toes. If he runs with his heels hitting the ground his head will go up and down and every fly ball will look to him as though it's a yo-yo.

When an outfielder has to play the "sun field" (with the sun full in his face), he should block out the sun's rays with the outstretched palm of the bare hand from the time the pitcher starts the windup until the play is concluded.

The line drive gives the outfielder the most trouble. When

they are in front, they sink fast. When they're to the side and overhead, they curve. And, of course, they travel!

As the outfielder drives in for a low liner, he's got to make a decision: Can I catch it? Or should I let it bounce? The score, the inning and whether there are runners on base weight this decision. If it's a tough chance and the defensive team is well ahead, it's worth a try. If two are out and none are on in the early innings and no score, again its obvious that the outfielder should make the try. But, if it's a tight ball game, he'd better play the bounce. If the ball gets by it might go for two or three bases.

When a right-handed batter lashes a liner to the outfield, it curves toward right field. A line drive off the bat of a left hand hitter curves toward left. Thus, when a line drive is hit directly over an outfielder's head, he should turn to his left if the hitter is right-handed and to his right if the hitter is lefthanded. That way, the ball will curve toward him and not away.

When an outfielder trots out to his position, he should do two things: Check the direction of the wind and check his position against those of the other outfielders.

More often than not, fields used by amateurs are not marked properly. Very seldom is the foul line extended beyond 1st or 3rd base. If this is the case, the right and left fielders, with the aid of the catcher, should mark the line next to their positions. (They can put a small stick in the ground and tie a handkerchief to it, or put a stone on top of a piece of white paper).

This is important, because an outfield makes its adjustments from the foul lines. With a right hand hitter at bat, for example, the outfield is usually adjusted from left to right. The left fielder stays close enough to this foul line to catch anything that's in fair territory. The center fielder stays close enough to the left fielder so that the two of them can cover all the territory in between. The right fielder then makes his adjustment with the same thought in mind. But, it all starts, you see, with the foul line.

## Leave One Hole

Under ordinary circumstances, the outfield plays so that only one "hole*'" is exposed to the hitter. If the outfield played at normal depth, and spread out so that all the territory between the foul lines was divided equally, four "holes" would exist for the hitter—along the left field line, in left-center, in right-center and along the right field line. To offset this, the outfield would normally "crowd" the left field line against a right hand hitter and the right field line against the left hand hitter. In this way, too, the one hole will be where the batter is least likely to hit the ball.

It's also generally true that the hitter will hit to the "opposite field" with less than average power. Obviously, then, the "opposite field" player—right fielder playing a right hand hitter, for example—should be in closer than the other two outfielders.

## "Togetherness"

The reader should begin to realize by now that the outfield plays as a unit and not as three individuals when a ball is hit by the batsman. The outfield not only makes adjustments before the ball is hit, as we've said, but during its flight and after it is reached by a fielder. Here are some examples:

When a ground ball is hit between two fielders, the nearest one should try to cut it off as quickly as possible. (Just as the third baseman tries to cut off the ground ball going between him and the shortstop). His teammate, on the other hand, should run deeper so that if the ball gets through the first outfielder it won't go any farther.

The center fielder makes the "call" on all balls hit to his right or left.

The outfielder makes the call on all fly balls dropping behind the infield.

Sometimes an extra base hit gets by an outfielder and rolls for some distance. The nearest outfielder should cut in between the infielder waiting for the relay and the boy chasing the ball. (Two relays in this situation).

Outfielders should back each other up on every play.

Each outfielder should back up the base in front of him on *every* infield play.

On a hit to right, the left fielder should move so he's on a line with a possible throw from right field to 2nd base.

On a hit to left, the right fielder should move so he's on a line with a possible throw from left field to 2nd base. .

The center fielder should back up all throws from the catcher or pitcher to 2nd base. (This applies to the catcher's practice throw to 2nd between innings).

## "Think Ahead-Be Ahead"

To keep runners from advancing freely, the outfielder must think ahead. With runners on base, he should know, before the pitch, just what he's going to do with the ball if it comes to him on the ground or on the fly. Junior league outfielders have more trouble with this aspect of play than any other. Yet, it's relatively simple. Usually, there is only one decision to make—IF the outfielder "reads" the situation in advance.

Let's try the easier ones first.

On all extra base hits—with one exception— the outfielder retrieving the ball throws to the relay man. The exception applies to the double with none on. The outfielder asks himself: "Can I get the runner going into 2nd, or can't I?" If the ball is not too deep and the outfielder is in good position, he might wish to throw directly to 2nd, instead of to the relay man.

With a runner on 1st base, the outfielder should realize, in advance, that the runner will try to go to 3rd on a single. Should he throw every ball he fields to 3rd? Of course not. If the ball is hit sharply and the outfielder makes a fast, clean pickup, he's got a chance. So he throws to 3rd. If the ball is not hit sharply and handled slowly, he throws to 2nd to keep the hitter from taking an additional base.

With a runner on 1st base, then, the outfielder again has but one decision to make—"do I have a chance at 3rd, or don't I?" With practice, he'll know the answer automatically.

With a runner on 2nd base, the outfielder knows a single may mean a score. Again, he has to make one decision— "can I get the man at the plate?"

With a runner on 1st and 2nd, the outfielder has an option —home, 3rd, or 2nd in that order. If he has a chance to prevent the runner on 2nd from scoring, he should fire away at the plate.

If he's in right field and he doesn't have a chance at the plate, he probably won't be able to get the runner going from 1st to 3rd either. So his throw wants to go to 2nd.

A slightly different situation presents itself to the left and center fielder, however. If they can't catch the runner at home, they should throw to 3rd. The runner on 1st will either be trying to make it to 3rd—and if he does, a throw from center or left should be good for a put-out—or he will hold at 2nd.

With the bases loaded, the outfielder ignores the runner on 3rd, as he will score easily on a base hit. He makes the play as though only 1st and 2nd were occupied.

On deep fly balls, the outfielder can expect a runner at 2nd or 3rd to "tag up" and try to advance after the catch. Again there is one decision—"can my throw reach the base ahead of the lead runner in time for a put-out?" If the answer is "yes," the outfielder makes his bid for the out. If not, he makes the throw ahead of the second runner, or simply returns the ball to the infield.

When the winning run is on 3rd late in the ball game, the outfielder should not attempt to catch a fly ball in foul territory unless he can surely keep the runner from scoring. If the outfielder is on the visiting team and the tying run is on 3rd in the ninth inning, he should also let the deep foul fly drop.

## "Field On One Hop. Throw On One Hop"

Like the line drive, the ground ball gives young outfielders a lot of trouble.

Most beginners will move in front of a ground ball and wait for it to come to wherever they stand. This bad habit should be broken quickly. The outfielder ought to realize this:

1. The longer it takes to reach the ball, the more distance the base runner covers.

2. The ball slows up with each bounce. As it loses force, the bounce becomes more erratic—so erratic it will often elude the outfielder just as he reaches for it.

Get to the ball as quickly as possible—don't wait for the ball to come to you. Whenever possible, field it on "one hop." That first bounce will be strong and true, the easiest to handle. Go get it!

If the ball has been hugging the ground for a long distance before reaching the outfielder, he must be extra careful so as not to let it go through his legs. Some outfielders turn the body sideways and drop to one knee to block the ball. Youngsters using this technique have a tendency to get down on the blocking knee too soon. Then, if the ball bounces a little off line as it reaches them, the outfielder can't move quickly enough to get in front of it After fielding the ball, the outfielder has to get to his feet to throw. The professionals can do it quickly and easily. This is not always true with boys.

To block the "grass cutter," youngsters are advised to use the trap position suggested for the third baseman. Get in front of the ball, drop to a deep squat with feet together, hands and elbows between the knees and glove on the ground.

When an outfielder throws to a base from normal depth to catch a runner, he has these objectives:

(a)  Throw the ball where the cut-off man can reach it.

(b)  Throw the ball so that the infielder at the base can receive it at knee height.

This can be accomplished by throwing the ball directly overhand to get the back spin and by throwing at the cut-off man's head. If the cut-off man is at the correct distance from the base, the ball will arrive with one bounce, just right for the tag play.

When the outfielder is close to the infield, however, he should throw "on the fly." The ball should be thrown hard and arrive about waist high. As a general rule, outfielders should always throw one base *ahead* of the runner, rarely behind.

PART III
INDIVIDUAL OFFENSE

Chapter 11

# Maneuvering On The Bases

The youngster learning to play baseball needs more instruction about conduct on the bases than one might suspect. Most are not aware of the fact that there are basic principles that can be applied to base running.

The base runner who flounders—makes a false start, back-pedals, starts again, then stops—usually does so for two reasons. First, he is inexperienced. Even if he's played a full season, it's possible, because of the nature of the game, that he may not have been confronted with a given situation more than once or twice—if at all! But the biggest factor of all is this: Our base runner has not analyzed the "situation" in ADVANCE. He should know, BEFORE THE PITCH, how many outs there are, the ball and strike count, and what he's going to do if the ball is hit on the ground, or in the air. This is not as difficult as it sounds. Consider, first of all, the simpler possibilities:

1. With two outs, the runner should leave the base at the crack of the bat—on *every* batted ball. If the batter flies out to center field, the inning is over. If he grounds out to 3rd, the inning is over. But if he smacks out a base hit, the runner may be on his way to score! The runner has everything to gain, nothing to lose.

2. If a runner is on 1st base with less than two out (or on any base in a force-play situation), he MUST run on a ground ball. His objective is to beat a possible throw to the base ahead of him, defeating any bid for a double, or even

(Note: This exercise is particularly good during indoor skull sessions. Here is how to read chart. "A ground ball is hit to fielder with none out. What do I do if I'm on 1st Base?"

## WHAT DO I DO IF I'M ON....

| | | 1st Base | 2nd Base | 3rd Base | 1st Base With Man On 2nd | 1st Base With Man On 3rd | 1st Base With Man On 2nd & 3rd | 2nd Base With Man On 1st | 2nd Base With Man On 3rd | 2nd Base With Man On 1st & 3rd | 3rd Base With Man On 2nd | 3rd Base With Man On 1st | 3rd Base With Man On 1st & 2nd |
|---|---|---|---|---|---|---|---|---|---|---|---|---|---|
| | | A | B | C | D | E | F | G | H | I | J | K | L |
| A GROUND BALL IS HIT TO A FIELDER WITH... | I None Out | Run | | | | | | | | | | | |
| | II One Out | Run | | | | | | | | | | | |
| | III Two Outs | Run | | | | | | | | | | | |
| A Fly Ball Is Hit To A Fielder With... | IV None Out | ½ Way | | | | | | | | | | | |
| | V One Out | ½ Way | | | | | | | | | | | |
| | VI Two Outs | Run | | | | | | | | | | | |

a triple play. If the runner hesitates in this situation, he makes it easy for the defense to execute the DP. On the other hand, if the ball goes *through* the infield, he could pick up an extra base—the one directly ahead of him and one more. And, again, that last one may be home plate! So, with no ifs, ands, or buts, we now have two MUST situations, as they are called.

### "Make The Ball Go Through"

Take a look at line I, column B on the chart on page 102. If you read the chart as suggested, you would say: The batter hits a ground ball with none out. I'm on 2nd base. What do I do?" Most young players would unhesitatingly light out for 3rd. If this player carried the tying or winning run in a championship game, the results might be pretty disastrous—especially if the ball were fielded by the third baseman or shortstop. For obviously, the shortstop or third baseman could easily make the put-out. If either did, the batter would be on 1st with two out, putting the team on offense much further away from the pennant than before.

The general principle to follow here is this: If you are on 2nd base with less than two out and a ground ball is hit to 3rd or short—hold up. The professionals say—"make the ball go through" (the infield) before advancing. If, on the other hand the ball is hit to 2nd or 1st, go and go hard!

Without looking up the answers on page 106, go through the chart and see how many other times this principle would apply to a baserunner on 2nd.

To explain further how a "situation" dictates the tactics a baserunner should use, take a look at line IV and apply it to columns A, B, C. If you're on 1st base and a ball is hit to the outfield, the runner, as indicated, should move half-way toward 2nd. Then, if the ball is caught, he can return to 1st. Mostly, he is guarding against the ball being dropped. For if it's dropped, he must hustle to 2nd to keep from being caught in a force-out. If he's on 2nd, however, the situation is much different. Second base is not too difficult a throw from the normal outfield position, so he cannot go half-way to 3rd, else the outfielder, after making the catch, will throw the ball behind the runner and double him off. This not only means an out, it means eliminating a runner from good scoring position. What should the runner do?

First, he must judge how deeply the ball has been hit. If it goes to the wall, he probably can make 3rd after the catch and should be prepared to do so. He would then be on 3rd with one out and could score in one of many ways. If the ball is at normal depth, though, it's best that he take a short lead—one that would enable him to get back to 2nd safely if the ball is caught, or offer him a *chance* to advance if the ball is dropped.

Move the runner to 3rd, now, with none out. If the fly ball is deep, the runner could score easily after the catch. Naturally, he would "tag-up" until the ball were caught. But, suppose the ball is at normal depth? The runner, if he chooses, could take a lead on the theory that if the ball were dropped, he could score. But a better practice would seem to be to "tag-up" and, after the catch, bluff a start for the plate. He might draw a throw to home. A bad bounce on that throw might mean a score. Furthermore, it's always good practice to keep pressure on the defense.

These techniques, by the way, apply to fly balls in the reach of the infielders, too. Very often, for example a second baseman will make a catch of a fly ball with his back to the plate—"going away". The runner on 3rd should be tagging up and *go* if the second baseman doesn't seem to be alert, or if he doesn't seem to be in a good position to throw.

There's one other situation on the chart that we might

examine—line I, column C. If a runner is on 3rd base and the batter hits a ground ball, should the runner stay, or go? Before deciding, consider these factors: Is the infield up or back? How hard is the ball hit? What is the score? What is the inning? These questions may seem confusing, but they really aren't. In the first place, the runner should *know* the inning, the score and the depth of the defense *before* the ball is pitched. In other words, he knows in *advance* what moves are open to him.

If the infield is back deep, the runner should have no trouble scoring on a ball hit to the right side. It might be close, however, if the ball is hit sharply and fielded on one bounce by either the shortstop or third baseman. (With the ball hit to the left side, much also depends on the speed of the runner and whether he is breaking with the pitch).

From a study of the chart and the preceding discussion, these general principles emerge:

1. If a base runner is in a force-play situation and the ball is hit on the ground, he must..... RUN!

2. If a base runner is on 2nd base with less than two out and a ground ball is hit in front of him, he should hold up until the ball goes "through"; if behind him ... RUN!

3. If a base runner is on 3rd with the infield back, he can run if the ball is hit to the right side. He must judge the sharpness of the hit and the "situation" if the ball is bounced to the left side.

4. The runner must use slightly different tactics at each base on fly balls with less than two out. ("Half way" when on 1st base; "tag-up" or lead from 2nd; *always* "tag-up" from 3rd).

5. With two outs, the runner must always *GO* on ANY KIND OF HIT.

Answers to chart on page 102

Line I—Column A, Run; Column B, If ball is behind, run. If ahead, hold up until ball goes through; Column C, judge situation advance. If infield is playing deep, for example, runner should go; Column D, run; Column E, run; Column F, run; Column G, run; Column H, If ball is behind, run. If ahead, hold up until ball goes through; Column I, run; Column J, Judge situation in advance and react accordingly; Column K, Same as C and J; Column L, run.

Line II—Column A, run; Column B, same as I-B; Column C, same as I-C; Column D, run; Column E, run; Column F, run; Column G, run; Column H, If ball is in front, make it go through. If behind, run; Column I, Run; Column J, must judge situation in advance. If infield is deep, run; Column K, Same as J; Column L, run.

Line III—Columns A to L, run.

Line IV—Column A, go halfway; Column B, tag up if ball is deep, short lead if shallow; Column C, tag up and go if ball is deep, bluff if shallow; Column D, halfway; Column E, halfway; Column F, halfway; Column G, tag up if ball is deep, short lead if shallow; Column H, same as G, but do not advance unless man on 3rd goes; Column I, same as H; Column J, tag up and go if ball is deep, bluff going if shallow; Column K, same as J; Column L, same as J.

Line  V—All answers same as Line III.

Line VI—Columns A to L, Run.

**Chapter 12**

# Leading Away and Stealing

A base runner can travel the 90 feet between bases in about three to four seconds. A ball can be thrown that same distance in less than one second. It is obvious then that any boy who wants to steal a base has his work cut out for him. Let's assume you are the runner now, and breakdown and examine the whole process of leading away, returning to the base, and breaking for the next base.

First of all, be sure the pitcher has his foot on the rubber before giving up contact with the base. As you wait for him to put his foot on the rubber, face the mound with your left foot against the rear corner of the base.

You can start leading away as the pitcher takes his stretch —but be careful! The pitcher can throw almost any time during the stretch move. (If the pitcher uses a full windup, you can move as soon as he moves).

To get away from the base, take a sliding step right with the right foot. Bring the toe of the left foot in back of right heel and take another sliding step right. You should be able to take three and a half such steps. (About the length of your body plus one step).

When you reach the end of your lead, the heels should be off the ground, the weight distributed evenly on the balls of both feet, the body bent at the waist, hands hanging free. Be poised to go either way.

*Never* turn your back on the base and walk away from

it to obtain a lead. *Never* lean, or shift too much weight in one direction.

## Leading Away From 1st Base

The offensive team should watch the opposing pitcher the first few times he takes the "stretch" position to pick up any weaknesses he might reveal.

Many young right-handers for example, will take a stretch, bring the hands to the stop position, then turn their shoulders to the left side as they look toward 1st. Before the pitcher can throw to the plate, he will have to rotate the shoulders to the right. Examine .this particular weakness— which is most common among young pitchers:

The pitcher takes his stretch. He turns head and shoulders left to look at the runner. As he starts to twist right, *that's* when the runner should GO! If the pitcher doesn't throw to the plate—and attempts to throw to 1st or 2nd instead —he will commit a balk and the runner gets 2nd base automatically.

But, balk, or no, the runner can get a tremendous "jump" on the pitcher by taking advantage of the extra move of the shoulders.

Assuming, however, that a pitcher knows his job and shows no faults in holding a runner, the runner should always watch the pitcher's feet—not the head or body. The feet will tell him whether to go back, or break for the next base. This is the way to "read" them: .  ' ", A right-hander who uses the "jump" move.

Watch both feet. If the front foot comes up—GO!

If the right heel comes up-GET BACK!

A right-hander who uses a pivot.

Watch the front foot only. If the front foot comes up and starts to the plate—GO! If it starts swinging to 1st— GET BACK!

A left-hand pitcher.

Watch the front foot only. It will come up, swing back then start either toward 1st or home. Don't move until you see which way it's going. But, don't take as big a lead as with right-handers.

Use these two methods to return to 1st base:

If it's going to be close—DIVE and tag the back of the base with the right hand.

If you have the throw beaten, pivot left, take the first step with the left foot. On reaching the bag, tag the corner with the left foot and at the same time swing the body right to face the infield. If the ball gets away from the first baseman, you're ready to go to 2nd.

When runner leading away from 1st has pick-off throw beaten, he should hit back corner of bag with left foot, let momentum swing him right.

## Leading Away From 2nd Base

As you lead away from 2nd, back into left field slightly. This will help you see the second basemen when you have your eyes on the pitcher. It will also hinder the shortstop as he races you back to the bag for a tag play. Take as much lead as the second baseman and shortstop will give you. If the second baseman is two feet away from the bag— you take two feet. If he and the shortstop are in normal fielding position—take three and a half to four steps. Don't turn your head to look at the shortstop. Listen to the 3rd base coach—hell tell you to "keep coming", to "stop", or "GO BACK!"

As far as the pitcher is concerned—watch both feet. If the front one comes up, you can go. If the back one moves, go back to 2nd.

Whenever you try to steal 3rd on a pitch, hook slide to the right. If you're returning to 2nd, go back head first if it's going to be close; or hook slide left or use the bent-leg straight in slide against the second baseman. Hook right or use the bent-leg straight in slide against the shortstop.

## Leading Away From 3rd Base

Sometimes the pitcher uses the stretch move with a runner on 3rd; sometimes the windup. If the pitcher is right-handed and takes a stretch, play him as though you were on 1st with a left-hand pitcher. If he's left-handed, play him as though you were on 1st with a right-hander.

If the pitcher uses the full windup, you're free to lead away at the *first move* of the pitcher's body—not before.

Always stand in foul ground when leading away from 3$^{rd}$ base. Thus, if you're hit with a batted ball, you will not be called out. Take as much territory as the third baseman will give you. If he's six feet away from the base, take a six-foot lead.

Don't try to steal home against a pitcher taking a stretch move; you'll never make it. If the pitcher uses a windup, take as big a lead as you can get, put your head down and *go* at the pitcher's first move—usually the hands. To get back to 3rd on a pick-off attempt, go head first if it's going to be close; hook left or use the bent-leg straight in slide if you have the throw beaten.

**Chapter 13**

# Reading the Signs

The Manager, and no one else, decides whether the team will bunt, hit-and-run, steal, etc. Usually stationed at the 3rd base coaching line (or on the bench), he uses either voice or body signals to tell batter and base runner what the play will be.

Whether a player is experienced, or inexperienced, he'll make the right move if he sees the Sign and understands it. But the sign is on and off in an instant. To catch it, *both* batter and runner have to be looking at the Manager at the proper time.

The natural spot for the giving of Signs is during the few moments before the pitcher gets on the rubber to start his throwing move. The batter—if we can concentrate on him before discussing either the runner or Manager—actually has control of the situation. If he expects a Sign, all he has to do is stay out of the batter's box and keep looking for it! As soon as he gets the Sign or becomes convinced no Sign is forthcoming, he should step into the box. (Caution: Don't step into the batter's box immediately after a sign is given. Let the 3rd base coach go, through at leas two additional motions.) At this point the pitcher will put his foot on the rubber and start his delivery. After the firs pitch (and each succeeding pitch), if the batter thinks a play might be coming, he should again step out of the batter's box and 'look".

The runner, too, has a definite procedure to follow in leagues in which "leading" is permitted. As the ball is being delivered, he should be moving off the base, ready to advance if the batter swings and connects. If the ball goes by the batter into the catcher's hands, however, the runner should quickly return to the base. As soon as the runner's foot strikes the base, he should turn and watch for a Sign. He should *keep watching* until the pitcher again puts his foot on the rubber. Once that happens, he should forget the Sign and concentrate on running.

In those junior leagues where the rules permit runners to take a 'lead", the players must remember this: *NEVER* leave the base until the pitcher has his foot on the rubber. If the pitcher is *off* the rubber, anybody could have the ball. It could be hidden in a glove, a back pocket or tucked under an arm pit. If our runner were off base looking intently for a Sign, that "anybody" could turn out to be somebody right behind him!

It should be clear now, that the Manager can only properly give Signs when he becomes aware that the batter is out of the batter's box, the runner is on base and the pitcher is off the rubber.

Try to catch them all—yours and those of the position.

**PART IV**
**TEAM DEFENSE**

Chapter 14

# The Bunt Defenses

When a baseball team is in the field, it must function as a *unit* to properly defend against the team at bat. When the ball is hit, *every* player on the defense has an assignment— a place to go, a maneuver to execute.

The fielders, of course, try to anticipate plays in *advance* and determine what will be done if a runner steals, if a pitch is bunted, if the batter lashes a hit to centerfield, etc. To make adjustments, the fielders consider several things: The kind of hitter at bat, the strength of the pitcher in relation to the hitter, the type of pitch to be used and the general strategic situation, such as the score and inning.

Take a look at some of the simpler aspects of Team Defense.

The Hitter: If the batter hits consistently to left, the infield and outfield should move a step or two toward left field. If the hitter is short and light of build, he probably hasn't much power. Bring the outfielders in two steps, the infielders in one step.

The Pitcher: Does the pitcher overpower most of the hitters? If so, the defense should move a step or two to right for right hand batters, a step or two to left for left hand batters. This move is made on the assumption that the hitters will be a little late with their swing against a strong pitcher. If the pitcher has average speed, but throws a lot of curve balls, the outfield should move up and toward left field a step or two. A hitter has to supply much of his own power when hitting the curve. He also will bring the bat around quicker.

The Situation: With a runner on 1st, none out and the score even, or the batting team ahead, the defense must be prepared for the Sacrifice Bunt. Specifically, the outfielders should be ready to back up the bases; the shortstop should be ready to go to 2nd, and the second baseman to 1st. The pitcher, catcher and the third and first basemen should get set to rush in on the bunt. The diagrams on pages 115-126 show the defensive positions that are taken to offset certain plays by the offense. Here is a word description of what occurs in each situation.

## The Sacrifice Bunt With Runners On 1st

In addition to the moves described in the preceding paragraph, it should be noted if the third baseman fields the ball, the catcher must swing to his left and go forward to cover 3rd.

The outfielders, on anticipating the bunt, move forward about three steps on the pitcher's downward swing. The left fielder, as soon as he is certain the ball will be bunted, circles to his right, running hard, until he comes to a point about 30 to 40 feet in back of 3rd. He's ready now to back up a throw to 3rd from anyone on the right field side of the diamond.

The centerfielder, after he's certain the ball will be bunted, charges to a point some 20 to 30 feet behind 2nd, where he can back up a throw to 2nd by the catcher, pitcher, third and first basemen.

The right fielder, after he's certain the ball will be bunted, makes a running circle to his left so that he will be some 30 to 40 feet behind 1st and in position to handle an overthrow to 1st. If he does pick up an overthrow, he can hold the batter at 1st and the lead runner to either 2nd or 3<sup>rd</sup>.

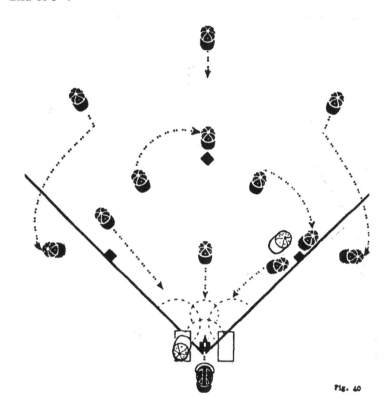

Fig. 40

Bunt defense with runner on 1st. If third baseman fields ball, catcher circles left after charging into diamond and continues along baseline to cover 3rd.

## The Sacrifice Bunt With A Runner On 1st And 2nd. (Or just 2nd)

The diagram on page 116 shows that the outfielders make the same moves when a batter sacrifices with runners on 1st and 2nd. The infield positions are different, however.

The pitcher is to field everything to his right to the foul line; the first baseman everything to the pitcher's left; the catcher anything he can reach in front of the dish.

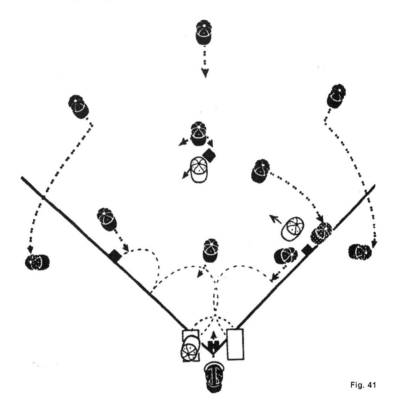

Fig. 41

**Bunt defense with men on 1st and 2nd (or 2nd only). Shortstop holds runner at bag before pitch, goes to normal position on pitch. If ball is bunted, he returns to bag.**

Remember that the objective of the offense in this situation is to bunt the ball past the pitcher so that the third baseman will be forced to field it. This protects the lead runner. If the pitcher fields the ball, the third baseman

pivots right and races back to the bag for a possible force*
out throw.

To help the situation, pitcher and shortstop should hold
the runner as close to 2nd as possible. (See page 86). The
second baseman holds his position until he is sure the ball
is going to be bunted, then he races to cover 1st.

## The Squeeze Bunt

The Squeeze Bunt defense is the same as that with a
runner on 1st base, with one notable exception. The shortstop covers 3rd instead of 2nd. If the ball is popped up, the
defense then can throw to 3rd and double up the runner
who was trying to score.

# Chapter 15

# Defending Against
# The Base Hit

When a runner is on 1st and a batter hits a single to right field the defensive unit swings to the positions diagrammed in Fig. 42. The centerfielder naturally moves to his left to help the right fielder either by backing up, or by calling the play. The left fielder moves in, to back up a possible throw to 2nd. The third baseman covers 3rd with the shortstop some 15 to 20 feet in front of him and in a direct line with the right fielder. The second baseman covers 2nd, the first baseman takes a cut-off position some 15 to 20 feet in front of the catcher but in a direct line with the right fielder. The pitcher, as soon as the ball is hit, runs to a spot at least 15 feet behind 3rd and in a direct line with the third baseman and the right fielder.

Once in position, this is what can happen:

If the hit is fielded cleanly and fast by the right fielder, he should fire at the shortstop's head. If the lead runner stops at 2nd, the ball is "one base ahead", as it should be. The shortstop, by the way, should cut the ball off.

Should the runner try to go to 3rd, the third baseman should yell "let it go" if the ball is on line and has a chance to beat the runner. If off line, or late, he yells "cut"! The shortstop catches the ball and throws to 2nd if the batter is headed there, holds it if he isn't. (You are successful if

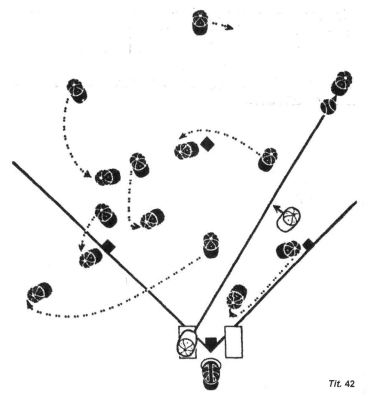

*Tit.* 42

Defending against single to RF with runner on 1st. Outfielder's throw should go to 3rd, or 2nd, depending on how quickly he handles hit. Note that defensive players are in position to back up both bases; that first baseman and shortstop are in cut-off positions.

you hold a runner to 3rd and 1st—better if you hold runners to 2nd and 1st).

If the hit to right field is soft and fielded slowly, the runner on 1st will have no trouble going to 3rd. The outfielder's throw will then go to 2nd to hold the batter on 1st. After catching the ball, the second baseman brings it to the mound.

Now, by putting the words and the diagram together, you can see that the defense is in good position to both make the play for the out, hold runners to the minimum number of bases and recover bad throws.

The same defense applies when the ball is singled to center, or left field.

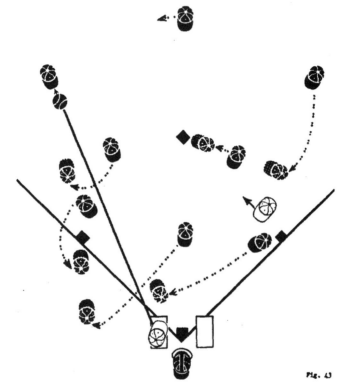

Fig. 43

**Single to LF with runner on 1st. Throw can go to 2nd or 3rd.**

### Single With Runner On 2nd

When a batter singles with a runner on 2nd, the runner will either try to score or stop at 3rd. The batter will

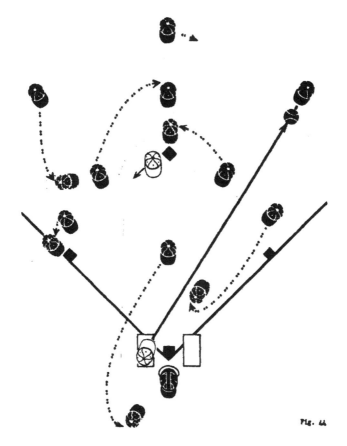

**Fig. 44**

Single to RF with runner on 2nd. Throw goes Home or to 2nd. Some
possible defensive moves not shown, however. If ball hit slowly to RF,
for example, shortstop might cover 2nd with second baseman playing
position as though bases were unoccupied. This diagram assumes ball
hit fairly hard.

either stop at 1st, or try to go to 2nd, depending on what
develops after the ball is picked up by the outfielder.

Take a look at the diagram on this page.

As you can see, the left fielder moves to back up 2nd as

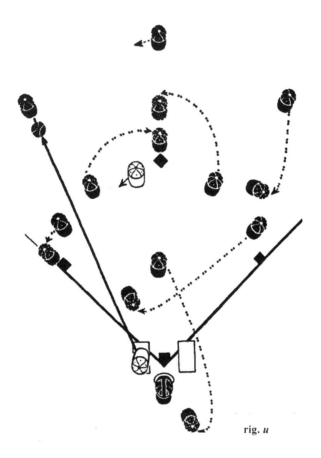

rig. *u*

**Single to LF with runner on 2nd. If throw is to plate, 1st baseman is in cut off position with pitcher backing up. If ball is cut off, throw goes to shortstop covering 2nd, with second baseman backing up.**

center aids man in right, the third baseman covers 3rd, the second baseman 2nd. The first baseman takes the cut-off position, the pitcher circles to the catcher's left to back up (to the right on hits to left). The Shortstop first backs up a possible throw from right field to 2nd. If the ball goes to the plate, he adjusts to back up a possible throw to 2nd from the first baseman at the cut-off position.

Here's what may happen: If the runner is trying to score and the outfielder fields the ball well, he will try to throw to the plate. If the ball is on line and ahead of the runner, the catcher calls for it. If late and off line, the first baseman cuts it. If the batter tries to go to 2nd, he'll be a dead duck on the first baseman's throw to 2nd. If he doesn't try to go to 2nd, the first baseman can carry the ball to the mound.

If the runner is clearly going to score, the right fielder throws to 2nd.

## With Runners On 1st And 2nd

The defense moves as it does with only 1st occupied— with one exception; the pitcher runs to a spot halfway between 3rd and Home. (See Fig. 46.) He then can move "to the play". If the outfield throws to 3rd, he can back up 3rd; if to Home, he can back up Home.

The outfielder, of course, has an additional option. If he's playing left or centerfield, he may ignore the runner trying to score from 2nd and try for the one going from 1st to 3rd. If both runners can easily advance two bases (2nd to Home and 1st to 3rd), the outfielder throws to 2nd to hold the batter at 1st. Whatever happens, the fielding unit is in a good position to defend and adjust.

When the bases are loaded and the batter singles, the defense ignores the man on 3rd—as he will score easily—and plays the ball as though only 1st and 2nd were occupied.

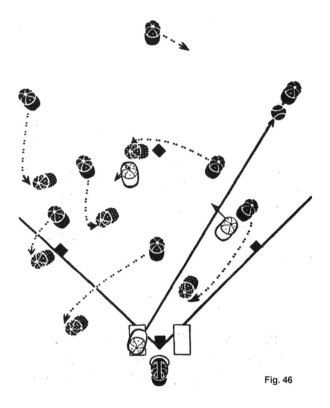

Fig. 46

**Single to RF with runners on 1st and 2nd. Throw can go to Home, 3rd or 2nd. If defense moves as indicated, cut off plays are made possible at Home arid 3rd and each base can be backed up by pitcher.**

### Extra Base Hits

On page 125 you will see diagrammed the defense for an extra base hit to right. The second baseman is out for the relay, shortstop takes 2nd, third baseman 3rd. If it looks like a triple, or double, the pitcher backs up 3rd, the left fielder 2nd.-Hie first baseman is in the cut-off position in front of the plate in case the runner tries to go all the way.

On extra base hits to left, the shortstop goes out for the relay, the second baseman takes 2nd, the pitcher again backs up 3rd (or home), while the right fielder protects against overthrows of 2nd.

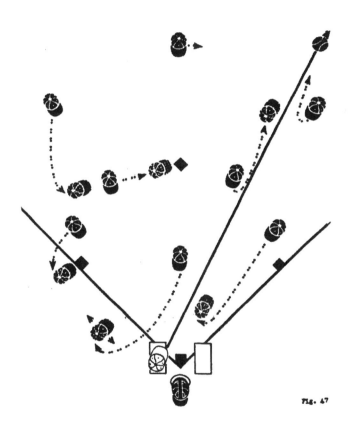

**Fig. 47**

**Extra base hit to RF. Relay man, on taking ball from outfielder, can throw Home, 3rd, or 2nd and each base can be backed up.**

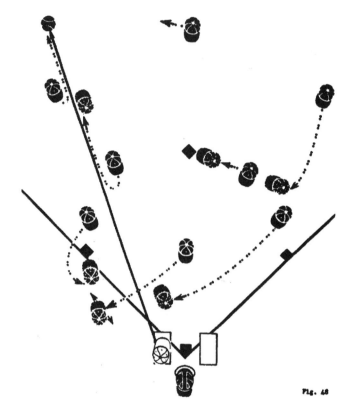

Fig. 48

**Extra base hit to LF.**

Chapter 16

# Tactical Defense

Now we come to some of the more complicated defensive decisions—what to do before the pitch when the bases are loaded, runners on 1st and 3rd, etc. Here again, the defense has to decide, in advance, what it is going to do. A situation-by-situation explanation may help your understanding of this problem.

The infield, first of all, can play at three depths—all the way back, which is as far back as it can go to make the average put-out at 1st on **a** ground ball; all the way "up", which is as far as it dare go to handle a hot smash and throw a runner out at the plate; "half-way," which is just between the two extremes.

Each depth presents certain advantages and disadvantages. When the infield is back, it doesn't have much of a chance to throw a runner out at the plate on a ground ball, if the ball is hit slowly, or bunted. But, it has more range to left or right and, of course, has a better chance to get die lead runner in a double play if the ball is hit hard. So, the infield has to decide, beforehand, which way it wants to go on a ground ball—to the plate, to 2nd, or to 1st. It adjusts accordingly.

In late innings, with the bases loaded and none out and the winning run on 3rd, the infield should be up tight. With one out—unless it's the last inning—the left side of the in field can be up for the left hand hitter, the right side back. Vice versa for a right hand hitter.

If the Home team were at bat, the infield might play up until one were out, then play back for the double play.

If the bases are loaded in the first inning, both teams would play back for the DP, conceding a run to the other team.

## Depth Of Outfield

The outfield, too, adjusts to the situation. With less than two out and the bases empty, the outfield plays at normal depth. With runners on, it might play a few steps closer to the plate to get a better chance to throw out the runner on a base hit, or hold a runner where he is on a fly ball. With two out, the outfield plays a little deeper than normal to cut down the potential of the "long ball". A single with two out, doesn't pose as much of a threat as a. double or triple.

When the score is tied in the bottom of the ninth with less than two out, and the winning run on 3rd, both outfield and infield play "in". The defense has but one chance to stay "alive"—keep the run on 3rd, or if the runner breaks for home, throw him out at the plate. After the first two put-outs, the infield can go back to normal depth, but the outfield should still play shallow—close enough to choke off a long single, and deep enough to catch up with the average fly ball.

# Chapter 17

# Defensive Signs and Pick-Offs

The second baseman and shortstop have the responsibility of keeping the outfield "informed" on each pitch. If no sign is given, the outfield can assume the catcher has called for a fast ball. If the catcher calls for a curve, the infielder might make some natural movement— a hitch of the belt, a kick at the dirt, a tug at the pant leg.

Up to the high school level, the relay of a catcher's sign to the outfield is not necessary, except on a pitch-out. The out is part of a defensive play used to catch a runner stealing, or to pick a runner off a base when he has too long a lead. The throw is always hurried and, with young bal players, often erratic. It is helpful if outfielders know in ad- yam ;e that a pitch-out, is to be attempted. As soon as the ball leaves the pitcher's hand, they can rush into back up The bases involved in the play. This relaying of the pitch out sign to the outfield should be started at the 13-year-old level; sooner if possible.

### The Pick-Off

There are pick-off plays for every base. Some are started by the catcher, some by the pitcher. Many are "natural" and do not follow a sign. The catcher's pick-off signs, like all signs, are not obvious. They might include a touch of the mask, a touch of the chest protector or a touch of the right knee. After a pick-off sign is given, the catcher calls for a pitch-out. He wants to keep the ball away from the hitter and, at the same time, be able to shift quickly into position for a clear throw.

Here are two common pick-off plays involving the catcher and started with a Sign:

There's a runner on 1st base with none out. The score is tied in the 7th inning. The situation calls for a bunt. The catcher gives the pick-off and pitch-out signs. The pitcher steps on the rubber, stretches and throws. As the pitcher makes his move, the first baseman charges the plate, the second baseman races to first, the right fielder runs in to back up 1st. The catcher steps clear, throws to the second baseman to catch the runner off 1st.

A similar play can be worked at 3rd base, with the third baseman charging in on the pitch and the shortstop going to the bag behind the runner to take the catcher's throw. The left fielder, of course, runs in to back up 3rd in the event of an overthrow.

## "Right Down The Alley"

The pitcher, too, can be involved in a pick-off play that starts with a Sign. This play, which is timed, is used when a runner is careless about leaving 2nd base. Professionals say that if the pitcher can see daylight between the runner and the shortstop—he's got an out. The daylight, of course, is to the 3rd base side of the shortstop. The out is obtained when the pitcher whirls and throws to the shortstop as he cuts to the bag from behind the runner. Few plays require as much teamwork as this one.

The sign, an extremely important part of the play, can be given by the shortstop, pitcher or catcher. When the short-stop is elected to give it, he usually does so by voice—by a phrase inserted in his regular line of infield chatter.

If timed correctly, the pitcher will be whirling to throw (on the count of "three") just as the shortstop is one step from the base. Shortstop and ball arrive at the same time. The runner* presumably, is caught flat-footed, or reacts too late.

It is recommended that the pitcher be designated as the player to give the signal for this play. He knows, better than anyone else, whether he can pick the runner off. He has better control of the situation than anyone else—and he's not forced to throw against his will.

Most shortstops are too eager to make this play and rarely are consistent about starting for the bag.

When the catcher is chosen to give the Sign, other difficulties crop up. If the pitcher is looking, the shortstop may not be. If the shortstop is looking, the pitcher may not be. Then, too, the centerfielder may miss the Sign.

Since a pitcher can't move any part of his body but his head while on the rubber (unless he's going to throw), he uses his head to give the Sign. Some pitchers do it with a significant head-bob. Others, after looking at the runner, turn their heads immediately to the plate if they're going to pitch. If they want the shortstop to go in behind the runner, they turn the head slowly away from the runner, then stare at 3rd. As soon as the pitcher's head stops in this quarter turn, the shortstop breaks for the bag and the pitcher starts his count.

Other pitchers, as they look at 3rd, very naturally lick their lips, or drop their chins. Either move means "go!" to the shortstop and centerfielder.

**Chapter 18**

# The Rundown

Sometimes when a runner is caught off base, whether it be by the pitcher, catcher, or any other member of the defensive team, he attempts to get free by dodging back and forth along the base line.

The team without a defense for these antics, is a team that's going to lose many a base runner, many an out, and, perhaps, many a ball game.

There is no excuse for a runner escaping, once caught in a run-up play. The defense has all the advantage. It need only remember these principles:

1. Take the initiative away from the runner
2. Put the runner out with no more than two throws
3. Put the runner out at the base he started from

Only three defensive players are ever needed to put a runner out once he is caught in a run-up. To help you comprehend what takes place, make a sketch of the diamond with each defensive player in position. You will see that you have five infielders with four bases to protect.

Now, put a runner halfway between 1st and 2nd.

The three players who would work together to put the runner out include second baseman, shortstop and first baseman.

Remove the trapped runner from between 1st and 2nd and put him between 2nd and 3rd. The three defensive men involved this time would be the second baseman, shortstop and third baseman.

Now place the trapped runner between home and 3rd. As you can see, the shortstop, third baseman and catcher make a handy trio for this side of the diamond.

There are more principles to be learned at this point and they involve the movements of each of the three-player combinations.

Here they are:

A. Whenever one defensive player throws the ball to another covering a base in a run-up play, he circles to his *right* to replace his teammate.

B. If the pick-off throw is behind the runner, the runner should be driven at least 2/3 of the way to the next base before a throw is made. The runner should then be driven back to the base he came from and put out with one throw.

C. If the pick-off throw is ahead of the runner, he should be driven back to the base he came from and put out with one throw.

## "Back Where He Came From"

Put our base runner between 1st and 2nd now, but fairly close to 1st. Assume that the pitcher has caught the, runner off with a quick throw to 1st. Here's what should happen:

The shortstop covers 2nd, the second baseman races to cover 1st. The third baseman stays at 3rd, the catcher Home. The first baseman forces the base runner at least two-thirds of the way to 2nd. He throws to the shortstop, circles to the right and comes in behind the shortstop to cover 2nd base.

After receiving the ball from the first baseman, the shortstop chases the runner all the way back toward 1st, until one throw to the second baseman will make the put-out.

Should the runner escape on the second throw, the rotation could start over again and continue indefinitely. This must be discouraged because the more the defense handles the ball, the more chance there is of dropping it.

If you look at the sketch again, you will see that no matter where you place a "trapped" runner and no matter which way you direct an imaginary pick-off throw, the three-man combination can work together to make the put-out as we have described it for 1st base.

There are three big advantages to this method—the defense uses a minimum number of throws for the put-out; every base is covered and the pitcher is not involved. The pitcher, however, should not be a spectator. When a runner is caught between 1st and 2nd, he should back up 1st. He should back up 3rd, when one is caught between 2nd and 3rd, and Home when a runner is being chased between Home and 3rd. (As usual, each outfielder backs up the base in front of his position.)

We should make a few more points before leaving this subject.

When circling right to rotate positions, go wide enough to avoid any possible contact with the runner in the base path.

In chasing a base runner, a fielder should not stop running or slow down to make a bluff throw. He should charge the base runner with all the speed. The runner, naturally, will try to retreat just as fast. Finally, when the ball is passed, he will have to check his momentum and get started in the other direction. *That's* when the defense should make the put-out!

Sometimes an outfielder or infielder will find a runner stopped halfway between bases. In this situation, the fielder should charge the runner, slightly favoring the base ahead. Force the runner to break hard in one direction or the other, then use the rundown tactics already described.

PART V

TEAM OFFENSE

Chapter 19

# The Percentages

Ball players say a team has to play "percentage baseball" to be successful. They're right. But, what is "percentage baseball?"

A Manager, first of all, is something like a checker player. As he directs the team on offense, he very often has a choice of moves. In a given situation, he knows from experience that move A has a better chance of succeeding than move B. If he makes move A, he's playing the "percentages." If he makes a different move, he's playing "against the percentages."

A number of factors affect the percentages, including:

The position of the runners

The ball and strike count

The inning

The score

The strength of the Pitcher

The strength (or weakness) of the Batter

Examine, if you will, each of these factors.

## Runners

It's easier for a runner to score from 3rd base, than from 2nd, or 1st, or Home (when he is the batter). If the runner is on 3rd, he can score in one of many ways—a deep fly ball, a deep ground ball, any kind of a base hit, an infield error, a wild pitch or passed ball.

From 2nd, it's a little tougher. As a matter of fact, it will almost always take at least a good single to deliver the run.

And from 1st, it's tougher yet. The Offense will need nothing less than a good double.

From Home, only a Home Run will do the trick.

The percentage *position* is obvious.

## The Ball and Strike Count

If the count is 3 balls 0 strikes, what are the chances of the batter getting a walk? What are the pitcher's chances of getting a strike-out?

To be "even" in this situation, the batter could let two pitches go by. The odds are that one of them would be a Ball. To strike the batter out, on the other hand, the pitcher would have to throw three strikes in a row. Obviously, the odds again favor the Batter.

## The Inning

When a team first comes to bat in a nine-inning game, it will have at least 27 opportunities to score. If the first man up gets on base, an attempt to steal 2nd would be less risky than, say, in the ninth inning with the score tied and only 1 out left.

## The Score

It's the object of the offense to make every move possible that will *add* to the original 27 opportunities to score; the defense to keep the opportunities at the minimum.

When a team is behind 0-to-4, then, it cannot very well use the Sacrifice Bunt or take chances on the base paths, else it will be aiding the defense. If a team is ahead, however, it can risk giving away an out here and there to put a runner on base, or to advance runners.

## The Strength of the Pitcher

If the pitcher has just walked three men in a row, would you expect him to suddenly regain his control and pour three consecutive strikes over the plate? Hardly. A good "percentage" play would be a "take" on the first strike pitched to the fourth batter. If the pitch is a strike, the batter is still not too bad off. If the pitch is a ball, the pitcher then has to throw at least twice more to get the batter out.

If, on the other hand, the batter swung on the first pitch, the inning—depending on die number of outs—could be over.

The "percentage" here is to make an obviously "wild" pitcher throw as many pitches as possible. There's no risk involved when a run is "walked" in.

## The Strength of the Batter

The percentage move with regard to batters is not too hard to judge. In a squeeze bunt situation, the question is, simply: "can the boy at bat bunt?" If the boy is a poor bunter, but a fairly reliable hitter, the percentage would seem to be to "hit away."

With the percentages in mind, now, go on to the next chapter. Check the list of offensive plays and take a look at how, when and why they would be used under normal circumstances.

# Chapter 20

# The Sacrifice
# And Squeeze Bunts

### *Objective*

The Manager signals for the Sacrifice Bunt when he wants to move one or two runs into the best possible scoring position and is willing to give up an out to do so.

### *How it is Executed*

With only 1st base occupied, it's best to place the ball along the base lines in such a way as to eliminate the possibility of a play at 2nd.

With 1st and 2nd occupied, the bunt should be made up the 3rd base line and hard enough to get by the pitcher. This will force the third baseman to field the ball, eliminating the possibility of a play at 3rd and usually 2nd.

The runner takes a good lead, moves off with the pitch slightly. He does not attempt to advance until the ball is ON *THE GROUND!*

### *When it is Executed*

Visiting Team—The Bunt sign can be given when the game has progressed past the middle innings; the score is tied or the visiting team is ahead; when there are none out with runners on 1st, and 1st and 2nd. It should be given when the batter first comes to the plate.

Home Team—Same principles as those that apply to the Visiting Team with one exception—the Sacrifice could be used to tie the score in the late innings.

## The Squeeze

### *Objective*

The Manager signals for the Squeeze Bunt when he wants to score a runner from 3rd, or 2nd and 3rd and is willing to give up an out to do so.

### *How it is Executed*

The batter gets as far back in the batter's box as possible.

At the last possible moment, the batter faces the pitcher and bunts the ball on the ground in any direction that is *away* from the pitcher,

The runner on 3rd can use what is known as the "suicide" squeeze, or "safety" squeeze. In amateur ball, the suicide squeeze is most common. The runner forgets that the batter is going to bunt and tries to steal home. He first takes as much lead as he can get (in foul territory). He breaks for the plate the instant the pitcher starts his normal windup. (In pro ball, the runner doesn't break until the pitcher turns his head to the plate to deliver the ball.)

During the safety squeeze, the runner goes about 1/3 of the way home on the pitch, waits for the ball to be bunted. If he doesn't think he can make it safely, or if the ball is popped up, or missed, he races back to 3rd.

When there are runners on 2nd and 3rd, (the Double Squeeze), some slight variations are employed. The runner on 3rd, takes a good lead, waits for the pitcher to turn his head to the plate, then tries to steal Home. The runner on 2nd takes a good lead and digs for 3rd as soon as the pitcher starts his move. If the ball is bunted, he rounds 3rd and keeps going.

Remember, the runners "go" on the pitch that follows the Sign; the batter bunts the pitch that follows the Sign.

### *When it is Executed*

Do not use the squeeze unless you are *sure* to surprise the opposition.

Use the squeeze with 1 out, the pitcher behind on the ball and strike count, a strong pitcher on the mound and when in the last two innings of the ball game. The visiting team should only squeeze when ahead or when the score is tied. The Home team could squeeze to tie, to win, or to add to a lead.

### The Double Squeeze

This is a very effective play in amateur ball, but seldom used. After the fielder picks up the bunted ball, his back will be to the second runner and he will almost always go through with the throw to 1st to get the batter. The throw alone will permit the second runner to score.

**Chapter 21**

# The Hit - and - Run; Steal and Bunt - and - Run

*Objective*

The hit-and-run play is one of the best offensive plays in baseball. The team ft bat employs it to move the defense from its normal position and—if a base hit results—to give the base runner or runners an opportunity to take an extra base.

*How it is executed*

The runner or runners break for the next base as they would to steal. The batter swings at the pitch, good or bad. If the pitch is far outside, he throws the bat at it to protect the runner from the catcher's throw. The batter tries to hit the ball on the ground to the unprotected part of the infield.

*When it is executed*

The play is normally called when two are out, the score tied or the team at bat ahead, and the pitcher behind on the ball and strike count. (The play can also be used with less than two out if the team at bat is well ahead). The best count is 2 balls and 1 strike. With the count 3 balls and 1 strike, the manager can sign for the steal. Thus, if the ball is over the plate, the batter will be swinging and the play will work just as though the hit-and-run sign were given. If the pitch is not a strike, the batter walks and the base runner or runners advance anyway.

## The Steal

### Objective

To advance a runner or runners without the aid of the batter.

### When it is Executed

As a general rule, the steal can be used:

By the Visiting team if it is leading, or the score is tied;

By the Home team if it is leading, or trailing by no more than one run;

When the runner, or runners are very fast and/or the pitcher, or catcher shows some weakness in playing their respective positions;

After one, or two outs have been made.

When the pitcher makes his first delivery, or is behind on the ball and strike count.

When any but the weakest hitter is at the plate.

## Bunt and Run

### Objective

This play is used to advance a base runner and put another run on the bases.

### How it is Executed

The runner, or runners, break with the pitch. The batter bunts for the base hit.

### When it is Executed

The play is used with one out, runner on 1st, or runners on 1st and 3rd and the infield back. The team at bat should be ahead. If the team at bat has a good lead, the play can be used during any inning. If the lead is slim, it should be used only in the early or middle innings. The bunt should be made toward 1st or 3rd.

**Chapter 22**

# Giving the Signs

Ball players and managers "talk" with each other through the use of signals, which may be given by voice, or by body movements. However they're given, the "Signs" should be both simple and complicated; simple for the team using them, complicated for the opposition. That's a contradiction, of course. The point is this: a team cannot use a set of signals that are hard to "read" or someone will surely miss one at a crucial moment. On the other hand, they cannot be so easy to read that the opposing team can steal them.

There's a neat way of getting around this, rest assured. But, let's take a look at what some of these signs might be, keeping in mind that any one might be associated with a play, such as the Bunt, Steal, Hit-and-Run, etc.

If the 3rd base coach is giving the Signs—and he's the best person to do it because he can be seen easily by the batter and base runner—he might:

Touch the peak of his cap with the right hand (left hand or both hands)

Touch the letters of his uniform shirt with his right hand (left hand or both hands).

Tug his belt with his right hand (left hand or both hands).

Move his right hand downward over right thigh (left hand or both hands).

Put flesh-against-flesh (clap hands, rub hands together, touch face with hand).

Turn back to hitter and walk away.

Put both hands on knees (or hips).

Call out batter's last name (or runner's).

Touch right elbow with left hand (or left elbow with right hand).

Cup hands to mouth and flash teeth at hitter or runner.

"Use A Key"

To help the situation, the manager might give the Sign with the right hand. Thus, any similar move with the left hand would be meaningless. To make it really difficult for the opposition, the manager should have a "key", or "build-up" sign. In other words, the genuine signal follows, or precedes the key signal. Let's say, for example, that two hands to the peak of the cap is the key. Any sign given before two hands go to the cap do not count. The first one following does. Assuming that touching the letters with the right hand means "take", look at what can be done in a hypothetical situation:

There's a runner on 1st base, with none out. The score is tied in the 7th inning. You are the home team. The situation calls for a bunt and the defense expects it.

Before the batter steps into the batter's box, the coach quickly goes through these motions:

Left hand to the hat. Right hand to the hat. Left hand to the belt. Right hand down the thigh. Stops giving Signs.

The batter steps in, the pitcher throws and its Ball One. The batter steps out.

**From left to right: False Sign; the "Key"; Bunt!**

The coach at 3rd, touches the cap with the left hand. The belt with the left hand. Both hands go to the cap. The left hand goes to the belt. The right hand goes to the letters. The left hand goes down the thigh. The signs stop.

The "take" is now on.

If the pitch is a Ball, the coach might give the "take" again. If it's a Strike, he could then give the Bunt.

If the opposition is stealing signals, it isn't necessary to change them—change the key. The key, by the way, need not be a hand sign. The manager, for example, could give the Signs that are genuine while standing at the home plate side of 3rd base. If he were on the outfield side of 3rd and gave the same signs, they would not be in effect.

We reiterate: Use signs that are simple, natural and distinct. Use a simple key. Change the key as often as you like, try not to change the Signs.

Managers should start using Signs when players reach 11 years of age. That doesn't mean a manager need expect his boys to learn all the offensive plays we've covered, nor does he need to give very many Signs. But any start made in this direction is helpful. The offense cannot function without direction. That direction has to be given through the use of Signs.

Signs can be taught in a gymnasium or in a private home before the season starts. All the manager need do is stand in front of the group and go through the moves—first without the key, then with the key. As the Sign is given the boys can sing it out—"bunt", "hit-and-run", "steal", whatever the case may be.

Boys should also be taught to watch for Signs while sitting on the bench. If the boys are missing Signs, the manager might institute a "fine" system—a lap around the field for every Sign missed.

# Chapter 23

# Coaching the Bases

Good baseline coaches are invaluable. They are particularly important to the younger players. When a 10-year-old gets on base, he's too inexperienced and too excited to do much thinking about his next move. He needs calm, clear, concise instruction.

At the higher age levels, the base runner needs just as much instruction and assistance because the game is getting faster and more complicated.

The baseline coaches have three basic tasks:

1. Direct the traffic on the base paths
2. Keep the base runners alert to the tactical situation
3. Give Signs

The most important "traffic cop" is, of course, stationed at 3rd, some 15 feet in foul territory. When the ball is out of a runner's line of vision, the coach, through the use of hand and arm signals, tells him what to do—slide, round-the-base, stop on the base, or go on to the next base. Here's a set of signals that is simple and distinct:

Slide!

Coach extends both arms downward with palms facing the ground, (to the left if he wants runner to slide left, to right if slide is to be to the right).

Take a Turn!

Coach extends left arm over head with palm facing runner. He extends right arm toward runner and rapidly cranks right hand in small circle.

Stop on the Base!
Coach points at the base.
Keep Going!
Coach swings right arm in full circle.

The 3rd base coach should always adjust to the position of the oncoming base runner, so that he is constantly in the runner's line of vision. As the runner circles toward 3rd, for example, the coach should go down the base line toward home plate, keeping well in front of the runner.

After waving one runner on, the coach should immediately look for the next one and not turn to see whether the boy who just passed has scored.

There is some traffic direction involved at 1st base, too. Especially on ground balls hit to the left side. The batter, after taking that first look at the ball, should have his eyes glued on the 1st base area and concentrate on running. If the coach makes no sign, he assumes the play will be close and that he has to run "through" the base.

If, however, the ball has gone through the infield, the first base coach should make several quick arm jabs toward 2nd as though to say: "Go there! Go there!"

One other person coaches base runners. He's the "on deck" batter, the boy next scheduled to hit. He has the very important assignment of coaching the runner racing from 3rd to home.

## Talking To The Runner

Once a runner gets on base—and before the pitcher takes to the rubber— the baseline coach should quickly go over the situation, like this:

"There's one out. Go hard on a ground ball. Go halfway on a fly. Don't take too much of a lead. Watch out for line drives!"

**PART VI**
**TEAM ORGANIZATION AND DEVELOPMENT**

# Chapter 24

# Matching Players With Positions

Until a boy gets to be 13 or 14 years old, it's usually pretty difficult to decide, in a final sense, the position he's best suited to play. At eight, he may look like a good 1st base prospect. At 12, because of physical changes alone, he may look more like an outfielder. It's a definite mistake to say early in a player's life that he's going to be a pitcher and nothing else. Even in the Major Leagues there are many examples of players being changed from one position to another.

In a group of eight-year-olds, only one or two boys are likely to have any stand-out ability. The others will perform at about the same level. As this group gets older, there will be some slight changes in every boy.

How, then, does the manager know which boy is best suited for 1st base, 2nd or 3rd? What should he look for as the boys go through their paces?

The first thing any manager should do is evaluate his material. He knows his boys have to run, hit and throw. He knows they have to field. All right then, who are the fastest runners? The best fielders on ground balls? On fly balls? Which boys have the best throwing arms?

If the first practice session is in the gymnasium, the manager can pick out the fastest runners immediately. If outdoors, he can quickly find out who can run and who can throw. To find the best runners, simply line the boys up in groups and race them! To find the best throwers, mark a throwing line at one end of the field and put markers at 50-foot depth intervals at the other. Mark down on a rating sheet which boys throw the farthest, (also, which boys run the fastest). At the start of this test, by the way, the manager would do well to emphasize the need to throw the ball on a straight horizontal line and not with a high arc. To drive home the point, he might say something like this:

"There's two ways of throwing the ball 100 feet. If you throw it straight up 50 feet, it will come down 50 feet and that adds up to 100. But runners don't run up, or down, but along the ground. If you want to catch a runner, throw the ball on a line and throw it hard."

Once the manager knows which boys can run and throw and which one's can't, he can start thinking about each boy's defensive assignment. Obviously, he's not going to find a boy with ideal qualifications for each position. He must make the best of the material in the squad.

Here are some things he might consider:

## The Outfield

In the outfield, the manager should first look for the boys who are steady on fly balls. Say he finds five of equal ability in this department. Of the five, which three are the best runners? Which three throw the best? Assuming that he has selected three, he must now pick his centerfielder, the most important member of the trio. This boy wants to be the fastest, because he's required to cover the most ground.

In professional baseball, the right and left fielders may have equal fielding ability, but the man with the strongest arm always plays in right as he has more long throw possibilities than the left fielder. In amateur ball, especially in the younger groups, the throwing ability of the right fielder is of less importance. And since more balls are hit to left, it's wiser to put the second-best outfielder in left, the weakest in right.

The manager, in building his outfield, should give as much attention to a No. 4 outfielder as to his regulars. The No. 4 boy will have to know how to fill in at all three outfield spots (other factors might dictate other methods of making outfield substitutions).

## The Infield

Selecting players to fill the infield positions is a lot more difficult than picking outfielders because the playing requirements are different at each spot and somewhat specialized.

The two boys who are the fastest runners, have the quickest actions and are steadiest on ground balls should be considered for the 2nd base and shortstop positions. The boy with the strongest arm should be at short.

The boy who is equally steady on ground balls, but perhaps a little slower afoot, would make the 3rd base possibility.

At 1st base, a number of qualifications are desirable. First of all, the boy who takes over this spot wants to be able to catch the ball with as close to 100% consistency as possible—whether throws are good or bad. The manager should look for a big boy. The big fellow makes a better target for the infielder and has more "reach."

The first baseman also wants to be steady on ground balls. He need not be a speed boy, however. As a matter of fact, if there's a boy on the squad who doesn't run well, but can field grounders and can catch the ball with reasonable regularity, he should stick to 1st base, or consider catching.

The left-handed first baseman has some advantage over the right-hander, all other abilities being equal. It's easier for him to make the 1st-to-2nd-to-1st double play and its easier for him to hold a runner on 1st base. Since the left hand thrower is normally only considered for 1st and outfield play, he should be carefully tested.

Behind the plate, of course, we need another boy with rather special talents. In the younger groups, size isn't too much of a factor. Neither is speed. But the catcher, like the first baseman, must be able to catch the ball consistently. He must also have enough courage to feel comfortable in back of the plate and be able to throw hard and accurately.

There's more to catching, however, than meeting the physical requirements. The catcher "quarterbacks" the defense. He's got to be one of the smartest boys on the club, and he has to be aggressive enough to direct the team effectively when it's in the field.

Since pitching gives the team from 70 to 90% of its defensive strength, the manager would do well to spend a lot of time looking for hurling prospects. In a sense, it's not too difficult. He can almost eliminate running ability and size. Highest on the list of qualifications is power and accuracy in throwing. Next, and often overlooked, it temperament. This is particularly important in the younger boys. The lower the class of ball, the greater the number of defensive errors. And the greater the number of errors, the tougher it is for a pitcher to win. The young pitcher, it must be remembered, takes his losses pretty seriously.

Our pitcher also wants to be able to think rapidly and be fairly quick and steady on ground balls.

## The Batting Order

The base hit, of course, is every ball club's major run-producing weapon. When a team goes to bat, the manager wants his players to bang out as many hits as possible before the defense can complete three-put-outs. And since the first half of the batting order will come to bat more often than the last half, it is obvious that the "top of the order" should be populated by the team's best hitters.

Batters, however, have different characteristics. Some hit for distance, but not consistently. Some hit consistently, but without much power. Some batters have great speed afoot, others are slow. The manager, then, must carefully evaluate the potential of each batter when he fills out the lineup card.

Theoretically, the order wants to look something like this:

1.  The boy who is apt to get on base more consistently than any other. (Power not a requisite).
2.  Another boy who can get on base consistently and one who is also a good bunter.
3.  The team's fastest long ball hitter and the boy with the highest batting average.
4.  A power hitter, but one who does not have to be as consistent or as fast as No. 3.
5.  Another power hitter, but one who does not have to be as consistent or as fast as No. 4.

The next four hitters should be ranked according to ability, with the best boy batting sixth and the poorest batting ninth.

In amateur ball, bat the pitcher where he will do the club the most good.

## Shaping The Attack

The material on hand tells the manager what kind of attack to use. If the team is weak at bat, but runs well, the club should bunt, steal and use the hit-and-run at every opportunity. If, on the other hand, the hitters are consistent, but slow afoot, the manager should "play for the big inning"; he should not rely on the sacrifice, or steal, but put all his chips on the base hit.

## The Substitute

Manager and players alike must remember that few, if any, pennants are won with a weak bunch. The manager should give substitutes as much attention as his regulars.

The defensive strength of any baseball team is "up the middle"; meaning catcher, pitcher, the second base combo and center field. Since the manager in amateur ball probably isn't going to have a replacement for every position, it's important to keep this principle in mind. He cannot do without two catchers, three pitchers, alternates at 2nd and short and a reliable sub for the centerfielder.

## Coaches

Most physical education people will agree that of all the major American sports, baseball is by far the toughest to teach. That's because the game is so highly skilled and because so many skills are involved.

To operate a team successfully and efficiently, the manager, whether he be in professional or amateur ball, needs the help of assistants. The junior league manager needs at least two. In general, the coaches want to be able to:

1. Attend all practice sessions and games.
2. Teach what the manager wants taught.
3. Instill confidence in players and win the confidence of players.

If the manager expects to keep volunteer assistants through the season, he should plan the program so that the coaches have something constructive to contribute at *every* practice session and game.

# Chapter 25

# Practice Sessions

To get the baseball program started—and it's never too early—the manager first needs to know:

1. What indoor and outdoor facilities are available?

2. How many assistants will be available?

3. How much time can be devoted to the pre-season program by the players, coaches and manager? How much time can be devoted to the program when the season is in progress.

### Indoor Meetings

Since so much teaching is involved in amateur baseball, work should be started indoors—in a gymnasium, classroom, or private home. The manager will find that there are many advantages to indoor work. He will be able to use visual aids, like movies, or slides. He can easily give written examinations and blackboard "chalk talks." He can schedule both daytime and evening meetings without worrying about bad weather. He'll also be able to teach many things he simply won't have time for once the playing season starts.

As a first step, the manager might jot down a list of subjects that can be covered at indoor meetings, keeping in mind the type of meeting place that will be available. He can then note the amount of time he thinks should be alloted each subject.

As a manager works out the schedule, he should remember that the attention span of a lively, growing boy will be very short. To get the most out of a meeting, the subject should be switched fairly rapidly. It is also wise to mix any physical activity with the "sit down" portions of the meeting and to change instructors as often as possible. At every meeting, the manager ought to try to review one subject and introduce a new one. "Review and add something new" is a good axiom.

After the practice schedule is made up, the manager can list the teaching tools needed—a blackboard, paper and pencils, white cardboard cut to the size of bases and home plate, rule books, tape to hold the bases in place, etc. The use of baseball equipment is not necessary and should be kept at a minimum.

Here's an outline of a program for a Babe Ruth team. It assumes the manager has secured a gym for an hour-and-a-half, once a week for four weeks.

*1st week*

Rules
Defensive Signs

Base Running
Hitting

*2nd week*
Rules and Review
Offensive Signs
Ease Running with Signs
Safety
2nd Base Pay
Catchers and Pitchers start
   work

*3rd week*
Rules and Review
Health
Sliding
Team Defense
Care of Equipment
Catchers and Pitchers

*4th week*
Rules and Review
Bunting
Team Offense
1st Base Play
Fielding Ground Balls
Catchers and Pitchers

The reader will note that "rules and review" top each list. This means that at least one or two rules should be discussed at each meeting and that one subject covered at a previous meeting should be quickly reviewed.

As the ball club gets ready to move out of doors, the manager makes up the second half of his program. Just as with the indoor meeting, he should first outline what is to be covered and then, as each practice comes up, write out the details. Here's a sample outline, which assumes that there will be four opportunities to practice.

| *1st meeting* | *2nd meeting* |
|---|---|
| Hitting (30 min.) | Hitting (30 min.) |
| Pitcher covers 1st (15 min.) | Stealing with pick-offs (15 min.) |
| Run bases (15 min.) | Run-downs (15 min.) |
| Fielding (30 min.) | Fielding (30 min.) |

| *3rd meeting* | *4th meeting* |
|---|---|
| Hitting (30 min.) | Hitting (30 min.) |
| Team Defense (15 min.) | Team Offense (15 min.) |
| Sliding (15 min.) | Bunting (15 min.) |
| Fielding (30 min.) | Fielding (30 min.) |

There are a number of advantages to organizing practice sessions in the manner described. First and foremost are these:

Time will be used efficiently.

Interest will not lag.

Players and coaches will know what is expected of them.

The ball club will eventually play up to its full capabilities.

If the manager is unable to attend practice, one of the coaches can carry on.

In running his practice, the manager should try to get

as much activity as possible to move along routinely. He should, for example, direct hitting and fielding practice exactly the same way at each meeting. Several suggestions are given in the following paragraphs.

## Hitting Practice

### *Pitchers*

If the club we've I been using as our model has three pitchers, allot 10 minutes to each boy. Have one boy on the mound, one warming up and the third in the batting order. The pitchers are to lay the ball in the strike zone at three-quarter speed. They are only to throw curves when instructed to do so. The pitchers should throw half of their pitches from the "stretch" position. They are not to bother fielding balls hit to either side. They are to keep the hitter busy. First two pitches are to be bunted fair on the 1st then 3rd base side of the mound.

### *Catchers*

Before the first pitch, the catcher goes up the 3rd base line about 15 feet and faces the hitter to field the bunt. He moves to the 1st base line for the second bunt.

### *Hitters*

Hitters should always bat in the order that would be used in a ball game. Two on-deck hitters should be clear of the plate with one on each side to retrieve foul balls. The boy who is to follow the 2nd on-deck hitter, should be in back of the mound keeping track of balls hit to the playing area. His job is to have a constant supply of balls on hand for the pitcher's use.

After the two bunts, hitters are given five *swings*—not hits. This discourages swings at bad pitches. On last hit, batter runs to 2nd, then back to his position. Batting order moves up.

## Outfield Drills

Managers waste valuable time when they hit fly balls directly to an outfielder—even a beginner. Make him run! For rapid improvement in outfielders, try this drill:

Take the outfielders behind 3rd and line them up one behind the other facing centerfield. Station someone in short center (perhaps one of the pitchers). Get another boy to assist the hitter (also stationed behind 3rd). At the hitter's signal, the first boy runs hard for centerfield, looking over his right shoulder. The hitter waits till the fielder is at least 100 feet out, then he whacks the ball so it will drop to a spot just in front of the fielder. If the hitter is inconsistent, he can forget the bat and simply throw the ball.

When the first outfielder gets to the ball, he throws to the relay man, who throws to the boy assisting the hitter. The outfielder continues to 1st base.

As the first boy gets close to the dropping ball, the second one starts.

All re-assemble behind 1st base. The drill is repeated with the outfielder looking over his left shoulder as he goes out.

The outfielders should then gather in centerfield and practice running straight in to catch the fly.

When working with the infield, the outfielder should make three throws to each base (except 1st). One ball should be hit on the ground to the outfielder. The others should be hit in the air to right and to left.

## Infield Drills

There is an established routine for the infield drill. It's designed to cover every possible play that would involve an infielder. Here's how the drill works, along with some suggestions for the manager:

### Get One

Initially, each infielder plays the ground ball as he would to retire the batter at 1st base. A second series has the objective of making the double play, 2nd-to-lst Finally, the infielders throw the ball home for a "force" at the plate.

Every time a ball ft hit to an infielder, he should cover his base to receive an eventual return throw from the catcher. Shortstop and second baseman should back up on balls hit to 3rd and 1st respectively.

To keep the infield drill going, the manager or coach should have two balls in reserve—one in his back pocket and one in the catcher's hands. Immediately after the manger hits one ball, the catcher should hand him another.

The manager should try to hit the underhalf of the ball to give it the big bounce. He should hit the ball to the left and right of the fielders.

On the first round the manager hits to the third baseman.

Third throws to 1st.

First throws to home. (Or back to 3rd)

Catcher throws to 3rd.

Third baseman throws home. (Or around the diamond via 2nd)

Batter hits to short.

Short throws to 1st.

First to home.

Home to shortstop covering 2nd (with second baseman backing up).

Shortstop to home. (Or to 3rd, then home).

Batters hits to 2nd

Second throws to 1st.

First throws home.

Catcher throws to 2nd. (With shortstop backing up)

Second baseman throws back to catcher. (Or 3rd)

Batter hits to 1st.

First throws to 2nd. (Shortstop covering)

Shortstop back to 1st. (With second baseman backing up)

First baseman throws Home.

(Home to 3rd and back to Home).

Batter rolls ball toward 1st.

Catcher picks up ball throws to 1st.

First baseman throws to plate.

Catcher throws to 3rd.

Ball goes "around the horn"—to 2nd, to 1st and Home.

## Get Two

Batter hits to 3rd.

Third baseman throws to 2nd.

Second baseman (covering bag) throws to 1st.

First baseman throws Home.

Catcher throws to 3rd.

Ball goes around the horn—2nd, 1st and Home.

Batter hits to short.

Short throws to second baseman covering bag.

Second baseman relays to 1st.

First baseman throws Home.

Catcher throws to short covering bag( second baseman backing up).

Short throws back Home (or around the diamond).

Batter hits to second baseman.

Second baseman throws to short at bag.

Short relays to 1st.

First baseman throws Home.

Catcher throws to second baseman covering bag. (Short backing up).

Second throws to 3rd (or Home).

Third throws Home.

Batter hits to first baseman.

First baseman throws to shortstop covering 2nd.

Shortstop fires back to 1st. (Second baseman backing up)

First baseman throws Home.

Catcher throws to 3rd.

Third baseman throws back Home (or around the diamond).

Batter rolls ball out for catcher (towards 1st, 3rd or pitcher's mound).

Catcher throws to shortstop covering 2nd.

Shortstop throws back to plate (or 1st).

Catcher throws to 3rd.

Third baseman throws back to catcher (or around the diamond).

On the final round, the batter hits the ball to infielders, who throw to catcher, knee high and over plate. After throwing ball to catcher, infielder charges plate. Catcher rolls ball toward him for another pickup and throw home. Either before or after drill, manager should give all infielders some practice on pop flies. Whenever possible during practice, manager might call out a hypothetical situation, give the infield 4 moment to think about it, then hit the ball.

For example, he might say:

"Bases are loaded. [None out. It's the first inning. No score."

The infield, without instruction, should play back for the DP.

## Phantom Infield Practice

To get a good look at the movements of the players—and to have some fun, incidentally—the manager should occasionally conduct infield practice without a ball. He swings hits bat at an imaginary ball; the fielders pretend to field it and go through all the motions of a regular infield drill. "Phantom" practice is particularly useful indoors. Sometimes it's used outdoors to amuse the crowd in the event there's a delay in the start of a ball game.

**Pre-Game Practice**

Practice before a game should be rigidly controlled by the home team. The visiting manager ought to be advised of the plans in advance. The time available pretty much controls the activity. It should be divided equally between Home and Visiting team. Normally, pre-game practice would function something like this:

Home team takes batting practice.

Visiting team takes batting practice, plus outfield and infield practice.

Home team takes outfield and infield practice and remains on diamond for start of game.

Each manager should see to it that his ball club is on and off the field within the allotted time.

**During the Ball Came**

While the pitcher takes his warm-up tosses, the first baseman, using an "infield ball," should throw ground balls to each infielder. The outfielders, with still another ball, should play catch to loosen up their arms.

As the pitcher gets to the end of his warm-up period (limited to one minute and eight pitches by the rules), the second baseman should cover 2nd with the shortstop and centerfielder backing up. The catcher throws to 2nd on the last warm-up pitch, then the ball goes around-the-horn. The third baseman is always the last man to handle the ball.

On strikeouts, (with the bases empty) the catcher starts the ball around-the-horn. On put-outs (with the bases empty), the last man to handle the ball, starts it around the infield. On a foul ball which takes a runner or a defensive player out of position, the infielders throw the ball around. Repeat: the third baseman is always the last man to handle the ball before it goes to the mound.

# INDEX

**A**

Attack, planning, the, 152, 153

**B**

Base hit, defenses for, 118-124
Base running
  leading away, 107-110
  principles, 105
Bases
  catcher covering, 59, 60, 63, 64
  outfielders, backing up, 97'
  pitcher, backing up, 49
  returning, to, 109
  running, the, 30, 31, 32-33
  second baseman, backing up, 81
  second baseman, covered by, 76, 77
  shortstop, backing up, 87
  shortstop, covered by, 85, 88
Batting
  guess hitting, 20
  hitting lanes, 20
  order, the, 152
  positions, arm and hand, 15
  stance, the, 13
  stride, the, 14
  swing, the, 16, 17
Bunt-and-Run, the, 142
Bunt, defenses, for, 113-117
Bunting
  hit, for, the, 23, 24
  sacrifice, the, 21-23, 138, 139
  squeeze, the, 139, 140

**C**

Catching
  equipment, wearing the, 65, 66
  infield, directing the, 65
  pitches, calling the, 60, 61
  pitchers, knowing the, 65
  positions, body and foot, 53, 54
  qualifications, for, the, 52, 53
  shifts, receiving when, 53-56
  signs, the, 62
  throw, the, 57, 58
Coaches, value of, 153
Coaching, bases, of, 146, 147

**D**

Defenses
  infield, adjustment by, 127, 128
  outfield, adjustment by, 128
Defense, strength of, 153

**E**

Extra base hit, defenses for, 124-126

**F**

Fielding
  "button" drill, 27, 28
  catcher, by, 58, 59
  feet, moving, of, 25, 26
  first baseman, by, 67-70
  fly chasing, 28
  ground balls, 26, 27
  outfielders, by, 93-95
  pitcher, by, 47, 48
  third baseman, by, 88-91

**H**

Hit-and-run, the, 141

**I**

Infielders, qualifications of, 150, 151

**K**

Key, sign, 144, 145

**O**

Outfielders
  adjustment, by, 95, 96
  defenses, by, 97-99
  objectives, of, 93
  qualifications, of, 149, 150
  steps, by, 93, 94
  throws, by, 98-100

P

Percentages
  batter, strength of, 137
  count, 136
  position, 135, 136
  pitcher, strength of, 137
  runner, applied, to, 136

Pick-off
  catcher, by, 130
  pitcher, by, 130, 131
  signs for, 129-131

Pitching
  best pitch, using the, 51
  deliveries, types of, 38
  grips, types of, 40
  head-bob, the, 44, 45, 47
  odds, 37
  pick-off moves, 44-47
  qualifications, 37, 38
  stretch, the, 43, 44
  strings, the, 41
  techniques, 39-43
  windup, the, 41, 42

Pitch-out, 129

Players, qualifications of, 148, 149

Practice, game, during, 162
  hitting, for, 157
  infield, for, 158-161
  outfield, for, 158
  planning, of, 154-156
  pre-game, 162

R

Rundown
  principles, applied to, 132, 133
  rotation, 133, 134
Runner, holding, the, 70, 71, 78

S

Second baseman
  cut-off play, by, 79
  double play, steps, by, 72-74
  double play, throw, by, 75
  fly ball, fielded, by, 75
  relays, by, 80, 81
Shortstop
  double play, steps, by, 83, 84
  double play, throw, by, 85
Signs
  defensive, 129-131
  examples, of, 143, 144
  offensive, 111, 112
Sliding
  hook, the, 34, 35
  leg-under, the, 34, 35
Steal, the, 142
Substitute, value of, 153

T

Tag plays
  catcher, by, 64
  first baseman, by, 71
  second baseman, by, 77
  third baseman, by, 92
Third baseman, position, of, 88
Throwing, drill, for, 28, 29

Also available from www.sunvillagepublications.com...

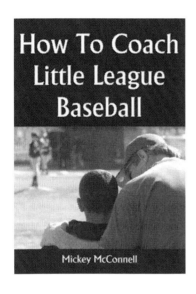

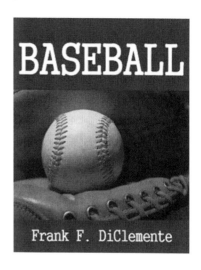

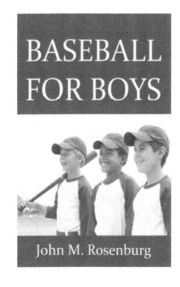

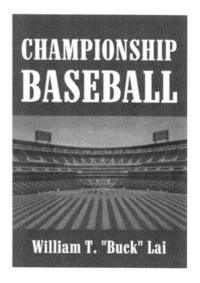

Made in the USA
Lexington, KY
09 June 2013